Simulations of Groundwater Flow and Particle Tracking Analysis in the Area Contributing Recharge to a Public-Supply Well near Tampa, Florida, 2002-05

By Christy A. Crandall, Leon J. Kauffman, Brian G. Katz, Patricia A. Metz, W. Scott McBride, and Marian P. Berndt

Prepared in cooperation with the
National Water-Quality Assessment Program Transport of Anthropogenic and Natural Contaminants (TANC) to Public-Supply Wells

Scientific Investigations Report 2008–5231

U.S. Department of the Interior
U.S. Geological Survey

U.S. Department of the Interior
KEN SALAZAR Secretary

U.S. Geological Survey
Suzette M. Kimball, Acting Director

U.S. Geological Survey, Reston, Virginia: 2009

For more information on the USGS—the Federal source for science about the Earth, its natural and living resources, natural hazards, and the environment, visit *http://www.usgs.gov* or call 1-888-ASK-USGS

For an overview of USGS information products, including maps, imagery, and publications, visit *http://www.usgs.gov/pubprod*

To order this and other USGS information products, visit *http://store.usgs.gov*

Suggested citation:

Crandall, C.A., Kauffman, L.J., Katz, B.G., Metz, P.A., McBride, W.S., and Berndt, M.P., 2009, Simulations of groundwater flow and particle tracking analysis in the area contributing recharge to a public-supply well near Tampa, Florida, 2002-05, U.S. Geological Survey Scientific Investigations Report 2008-5231, 53 p.

Foreword

The U.S. Geological Survey (USGS) is committed to providing the Nation with reliable scientific information that helps to enhance and protect the overall quality of life and that facilitates effective management of water, biological, energy, and mineral resources (http://www.usgs.gov/). Information on the Nation's water resources is critical to ensuring long-term availability of water that is safe for drinking and recreation and is suitable for industry, irrigation, and fish and wildlife. Population growth and increasing demands for water make the availability of that water, measured in terms of quantity and quality, even more essential to the long-term sustainability of our communities and ecosystems.

The USGS implemented the National Water-Quality Assessment (NAWQA) Program in 1991 to support national, regional, State, and local information needs and decisions related to water-quality management and policy (http://water.usgs.gov/nawqa). The NAWQA Program is designed to answer: What is the quality of our Nation's streams and ground water? How are conditions changing over time? How do natural features and human activities affect the quality of streams and ground water, and where are those effects most pronounced? By combining information on water chemistry, physical characteristics, stream habitat, and aquatic life, the NAWQA Program aims to provide science-based insights for current and emerging water issues and priorities. From 1991 to 2001, the NAWQA Program completed interdisciplinary assessments and established a baseline understanding of water-quality conditions in 51 of the Nation's river basins and aquifers, referred to as Study Units (http://water.usgs.gov/nawqa/studyu. html).

National and regional assessments are ongoing in the second decade (2001–2012) of the NAWQA Program as 42 of the 51 Study Units are selectively reassessed. These assessments extend the findings in the Study Units by determining water-quality status and trends at sites that have been consistently monitored for more than a decade, and filling critical gaps in characterizing the quality of surface water and ground water. For example, increased emphasis has been placed on assessing the quality of source water and finished water associated with many of the Nation's largest community water systems. During the second decade, NAWQA is addressing five national priority topics that build an understanding of how natural features and human activities affect water quality, and establish links between sources of contaminants, the transport of those contaminants through the hydrologic system, and the potential effects of contaminants on humans and aquatic ecosystems. Included are studies on the fate of agricultural chemicals, effects of urbanization on stream ecosystems, bioaccumulation of mercury in stream ecosystems, effects of nutrient enrichment on aquatic ecosystems, and transport of contaminants to public-supply wells. In addition, national syntheses of information on pesticides, volatile organic compounds (VOCs), nutrients, trace elements, and aquatic ecology are continuing.

The USGS aims to disseminate credible, timely, and relevant science information to address practical and effective water-resource management and strategies that protect and restore water quality. We hope this NAWQA publication will provide you with insights and information to meet your needs, and will foster increased citizen awareness and involvement in the protection and restoration of our Nation's waters.

The USGS recognizes that a national assessment by a single program cannot address all water-resource issues of interest. External coordination at all levels is critical for cost-effective management, regulation, and conservation of our Nation's water resources. The NAWQA Program, therefore, depends on advice and information from other agencies—Federal, State, regional, interstate, Tribal, and local—as well as nongovernmental organizations, industry, academia, and other stakeholder groups. Your assistance and suggestions are greatly appreciated.

Matthew C. Larsen
Associate Director for Water

Acknowledgments

The authors thank the City of Temple Terrace, Florida, for their cooperative support, especially Woody Garcia, former Director of Public Works for the City of Temple Terrace. Thanks are extended to Dana Carver of the Recreation Department and to the Public Works Department for the City of Temple Terrace for their generosity, assistance, and cooperation. The authors thank Eric Dehaven and the geophysical technicians at the Southwest Florida Water Management District for their help in obtaining pumping data and geophysical support and data during depth sampling of the selected public-supply well.

John Williams of the U.S. Geological Survey Office of Groundwater provided invaluable geophysical support and interpretation.

Contents

Figures

1. Map showing regional extent of the Floridan aquifer system, aquifer confinement status, major cities in Florida, and the TANC regional- and local-scale model boundaries in the Tampa Bay area 3

2. Map showing local-scale study area projected over the digital-orthographic-quarter quadrangle showing City of Temple Terrace boundary, nearby cities, springs, streams, gaging stations, and the selected public-supply well 5

3. Digital Elevation Model (DEM) of the local-scale study area with 20x exaggeration of vertical profile of the local-scale study area, showing the remnant Wicomico Terrace, numerous sinkholes projected from the DEM and the Northern Wetlands 6

4. Geologic and hydrogeologic stratigraphic column 8

5. Conceptual diagram of recharge, hydrogeology, and groundwater flow system dynamics for the local-scale study area 10

6. Diagram showing median measured water levels and simulated potentiometric surfaces of the surficial aquifer system and Upper Floridan aquifer in the local-scale study area, 2000 11

7. Map showing locations of wells and test holes installed for this study and trace of hydrogeologic sections *A-A'* and *B-B'* 12

8. Hydrogeologic sections across the study area 14

9. Graph showing median daily water levels from continuous water-level recorders in monitoring wells, stormwater retention ponds, and the Hillsborough River station, and various isolated measurements made in the local-scale study area, December 11, 2003 to November 17, 2005 16

10-14. Maps showing:
    10. Local-scale model area in relation to the regional-scale modeled area 18
    11. Distribution of recharge in the local-scale study area 21
    12. River and drain cells in the local-scale model and study areas 22
    13. Location of groundwater withdrawal wells and gaging stations in the local-scale study area 23
    14. Distribution of horizontal hydraulic conductivity in model layers 1 to 3, representing the surficial aquifer system 27

15. Graph showing the composite scaled sensitivity of the parameters used to calibrate the groundwater flow and transport model in UCODE 29

16. Graph showing simulated and measured hydraulic heads, hydraulic head gradients, sulfur hexafluoride and tritium concentrations, and corresponding weighted/nonweighted simulated and measured values 32

17-19. Maps showing:
    17. Simulated and measured hydraulic heads in the surficial aquifer system and intermediate confining unit in the middle of the local-scale model area 33
    18. Simulated and measured hydraulic heads in the Upper Floridan aquifer in the middle of the local-scale model area 34
    19. Simulated potentiometric surfaces of the surficial aquifer system and Upper Floridan aquifer in the local-scale model area 35

20. Graph showing calculated and measured sulfur hexafluoride concentrations in the selected public-supply well and monitoring wells 37

21. Graph showing calculated and measured tritium concentrations in the selected public-supply well and monitoring wells 39

Appendix Figures

Tables

Conversion Factors

Multiply	By	To obtain
Length		
centimeter (cm)	0.3937	inch (in.)
millimeter (mm)	0.03937	inch (in.)
meter (m)	3.281	foot (ft)
kilometer (km)	0.6214	mile (mi)
Area		
square kilometer (km^2)	247.1	acre
Volume		
liter (L)	33.82	ounce, fluid (fl. oz)
liter (L)	0.2642	gallon (gal)
Flow rate		
cubic meter per second (m^3/s)	70.07	acre-foot per day (acre-ft/d)
cubic meter per second (m^3/s)	35.31	cubic foot per second (ft^3/s)
cubic meter per day (m3/d)	35.31	cubic foot per day (ft^3/d)
cubic meter per day (m^3/d)	264.2	gallon per day (gal/d)
cubic meter per second (m^3/s)	22.83	million gallons per day (Mgal/d)
Hydraulic conductivity		
meter per day (m/d)	3.281	foot per day (ft/d)
Temperature		
degree Celsius (°C)	°F = (1.8 × °C) + 32	degree Fahrenheit (°F)

Vertical coordinate information is referenced to the North American Vertical Datum of 1988 (NAVD 88).
Horizontal coordinate information is referenced to the North American Datum of 1983 (NAD 83).
Elevation, as used in this report, refers to distance above the vertical datum.
Concentrations of chemical constituents in water are given in milligrams per liter (mg/L).

Acronyms and Abbreviations

ACR	area contributing recharge
cm/yr	centimeters per year
L/min	liters per minute
mg/L	milligrams per liter
NAWQA	National Water-Quality Assessment Program
PCE	tetrachloroethene
pptv	volume fraction, in parts per trillion
PSW	selected public-supply well
TANC	Transport of Anthropogenic and Natural Contaminants
TTP-4	selected public-supply well in Temple Terrace, Florida
TU	tritium units
VOC	volatile organic compounds

Simulations of Groundwater Flow and Particle Tracking Analysis in the Area Contributing Recharge to a Public-Supply Well near Tampa, Florida, 2002-05

By Christy A. Crandall, Leon J. Kauffman, Brian G. Katz, Patricia A. Metz, W. Scott McBride, and Marian P. Berndt

Abstract

Shallow ground water in the north-central Tampa Bay region, Florida, is affected by elevated nitrate concentrations, the presence of volatile organic compounds, and pesticides as a result of groundwater development and intensive urban land use. The region relies primarily on groundwater for drinking-water supplies. Sustainability of groundwater quality for public supply requires monitoring and understanding of the mechanisms controlling the vulnerability of public-supply wells to contamination. A single public-supply well was selected for intensive study based on the need to evaluate the dominant processes affecting the vulnerability of public-supply wells in the Upper Floridan aquifer in the City of Temple Terrace near Tampa, Florida, and the presence of a variety of chemical constituents in water from the well. A network of 29 monitoring wells was installed, and water and sediment samples were collected within the area contributing recharge to the selected public-supply well to support a detailed analysis of physical and chemical conditions and processes affecting the water chemistry in the well. A three-dimensional, steady-state groundwater flow model was developed to evaluate the age of groundwater reaching the well and to test hypotheses on the vulnerability of the well to nonpoint source input of nitrate.

Particle tracking data were used to calculate environmental tracer concentrations of tritium and sulfur hexafluoride and to calibrate traveltimes and compute flow paths and advective travel times in the model area. The traveltime of particles reaching the selected public-supply well ranged from less than 1 day to 127.0 years, with a median of 13.1 years; nearly 45 percent of the simulated particle ages were less than about 10 years. Nitrate concentrations, derived primarily from residential/commercial fertilizer use and atmospheric deposition, were highest (2.4 and 6.11 milligrams per liter as nitrogen, median and maximum, respectively) in shallow groundwater from the surficial aquifer system and lowest (less than the detection level of 0.06 milligram per liter) in the deeper Upper Floridan aquifer. Denitrification occurred near the interface of the surficial aquifer system and the underlying intermediate confining unit, within the intermediate confining unit, and within the Upper Floridan aquifer because of reducing conditions in this part of the flow system. However, simulations indicate that the rapid movement of water from the surficial aquifer system to the selected public-supply well through karst features (sinkholes) and conduit layers that bypass the denitrifying zones (short-circuits), coupled with high pumping rates, allow nitrate to reach the selected public-supply well in concentrations that resemble those of the overlying surficial aquifer system. Water from the surficial aquifer system with elevated concentrations of nitrate and low concentrations of some volatile organic compounds and pesticides is expected to continue moving into the selected public-supply well, because calculated flux-weighted concentrations indicate the proportion of young affected water contributing to the well is likely to remain relatively stable over time. The calculated nitrate concentration in the selected public-supply well indicates a lag of 1 to 10 years between peak concentrations of nonpoint source contaminants in recharge and appearance in the well.

Introduction

Groundwater provided public drinking-water supplies for 37 percent of the population of the United States in 2000 (Hutson and others, 2004). Within the State of Florida, the reliance on groundwater for drinking water is much greater—80 percent of the population (nearly 13 million people) relied on groundwater for publicly supplied drinking water in 2000. The percentage of Florida's population using publicly supplied drinking water from groundwater increased from 50 percent in 1950 to 80 percent in 2000 (Marella and Berndt, 2005). In 2000, 54 percent of the groundwater for public drinking water in Florida was supplied by the Floridan aquifer system. The Floridan aquifer system supplied public drinking water to 8.2 million people in four States (Alabama, Georgia, South Carolina, and Florida) in 2000 (Marella and Berndt, 2005). Nationwide, the Floridan aquifer system accounted for 8 percent of the groundwater withdrawn for publicly supplied drinking water (Maupin and Barber, 2005). One of the most densely populated areas in Florida relying on groundwater is the Tampa Bay area (fig. 1). In 2000, this area withdrew more than 1,135 million liters per day, with 74 percent of that from the Floridan aquifer system.

In 2001, the U.S. Geological Survey (USGS) National Water-Quality Assessment (NAWQA) Program, began an intensive study to assess the vulnerability of public-supply wells to contamination from a variety of compounds (Eberts and others, 2005). The Transport of Anthropogenic and Natural Contaminants (TANC) study is focusing on the transport and chemical processes of selected naturally occurring and anthropogenic contaminants from urban and agricultural sources within that part of the groundwater system contributing water to public-supply wells. Data collection for this study was completed in November 2005. Because subsurface processes and management practices differ among aquifers and public-water systems, public-supply wells in different parts of the Nation are not equally vulnerable to contamination, even where similar contaminant sources exist. The TANC study is identifying and comparing these important differences in a complementary set of aquifer systems, urban settings, and public-water systems based on data that were collected and analyzed using consistent methods. The northern part of the Tampa Bay region is one of the selected sites for a local-scale comprehensive study.

Purpose and Scope

The purpose of this report is to discuss the dominant processes affecting the vulnerability to contamination of a public-supply well in the Upper Floridan aquifer in the City of Temple Terrace near Tampa in north-central Florida. This report includes a brief description of the design of the local monitoring well network and methods of data collection and analysis. Groundwater ages and the distribution of selected constituents are used for developing basic interpretations of groundwater recharge and discharge patterns and pathways.

This report documents the construction and calibration of a local-scale groundwater flow model and the approaches used to refine a previously developed regional-scale model. The results of simulations of groundwater flow and traveltimes are also described. This report is intended to serve as a foundation for model synthesis analyses on which results can be compared between this TANC local-scale study area and other TANC study units in Connecticut, California, and Nebraska. Results of synthesis analyses and descriptions of other TANC study units are not included in this report.

Previous Studies

The hydrogeology of the Floridan aquifer system has been studied throughout its entire extent and locally in west-central Florida and the Tampa Bay region. Miller (1986) and Bush and Johnston (1988) characterized the hydrogeologic framework and hydrology of the Upper Floridan aquifer system throughout its regional extent, and Ryder (1985) characterized the hydrology of the Upper Floridan aquifer in west-central Florida. Stewart and others (1978) examined factors affecting the availability and quality of groundwater in the Temple Terrace area.

Current and historical surface-water data for southwestern Florida have been summarized in Coffin and Fletcher (2001). Flood profiles and historical information are discussed in Turner (1974) and by Goetz and others (1978) for the Hillsborough River Reservoir and by Murphy (1978) for Cypress Creek (a tributary to the Hillsborough River). Land use and historical discharge and nutrient loading to the lower Hillsborough River were discussed in Stoker and others (1996). Wolansky and Thompson (1987) described groundwater and surface-water interaction between the Hillsborough River and the Upper Floridan aquifer, and the Hillsborough River wetlands were characterized by Lewelling (2004).

Within the Tampa Bay region, groundwater flow models have been developed to study the groundwater flow system. A regional transient groundwater flow model was developed for the central-north Tampa Bay region by SDI Environmental Services, Inc. (1997). Langevin (1998) used this groundwater flow and particle tracking model, but added a fracture generator that increases transmissivities in fracture locations to approximate groundwater traveltimes in karst terrains. Yobbi (2000) optimized parameters for a steady-state version of this central-north Tampa Bay regional groundwater flow model, which was used as the initial model for the TANC regional-scale study. The regional-scale model was documented in a recent report on the hydrogeology of the Upper Floridan aquifer in the Tampa Bay region, which included regional information on climate, geology, hydrogeology, and water supply and the simulated contributing areas along with results of chemical analyses of groundwater (Crandall, 2007). The purpose of that regional-scale investigation was to identify major factors influencing contaminant occurrence and transport and to simulate areas contributing recharge (ACR) on a regional scale using an existing groundwater flow model.

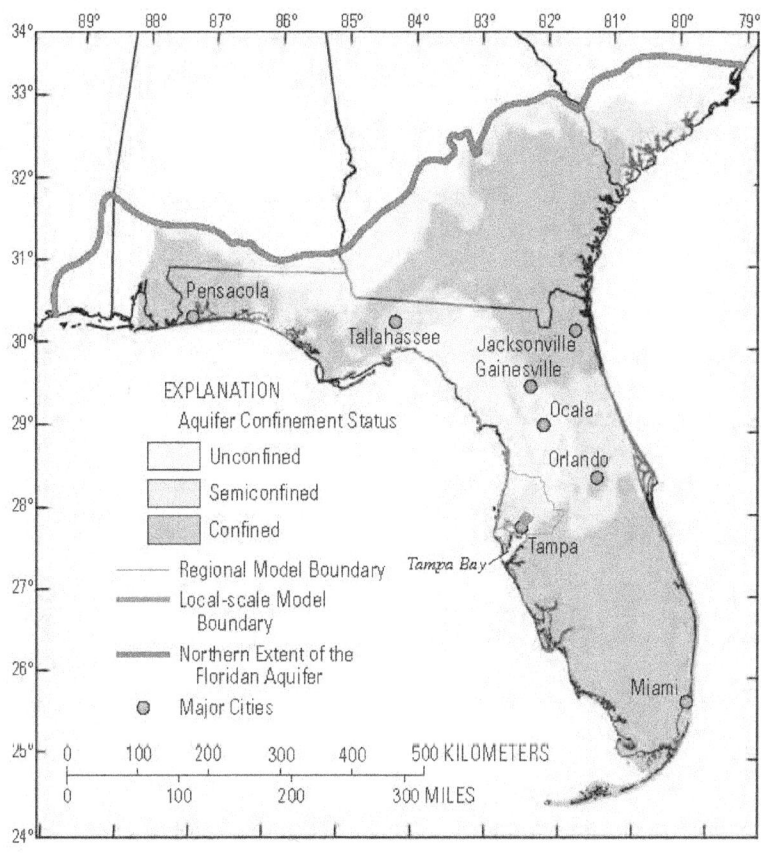

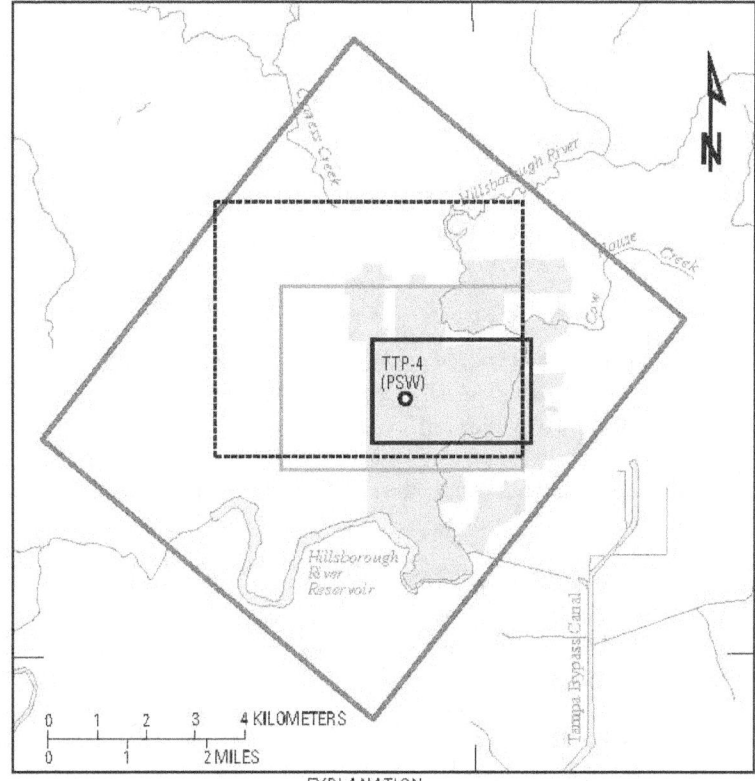

Figure 1. Regional extent of the Floridan aquifer system, aquifer confinement status, major cities in Florida, and the TANC regional- and local-scale model boundaries in the Tampa Bay area. TANC is Transport of Anthropogenic and Natural Contaminants.

Knochenmus and Robinson (1996) compiled results from numerous aquifer tests and other hydraulic tests in the Tampa Bay region. Initial measured values of hydraulic conductivity, which were used as the basis for simulated parameter values, were obtained from Knochenmus and Robinson (1996), Yobbi (2000), and the Florida Geological Survey (Jon Arthur, written commun., 2003). Knochenmus and Robinson (1996) also used various schemes to assess the effects of karst features on contributing area size, shape, and transport times. Sinkholes and their effect on water chemistry of the Upper Floridan aquifer were studied by Trommer (1987).

A study in New Jersey developed the general methodology applied by the TANC study to assess contaminant transport, ages, and flow paths (Kauffman and others, 1998; Stackelberg and others, 2000). A comparison of methods that assessed areas contributing recharge to wells was compiled by Franke and others (1998).

Description of Study Area

In 2002, a community water system public-supply well (TTP-4) in Temple Terrace, Florida, was selected as 1 of 30 wells which were sampled for the NAWQA Program's Source Water Quality Assessment study in the Tampa area. Water samples from this selected public-supply well (here-after referred to as the PSW) were initially collected and analyzed in the fall of 2002 for a wide suite of chemical and physical constituents. Results from the analyses showed the presence of multiple contaminants, but concentrations were below drinking-water standards. The analyses detected six volatile organic compounds (VOCs) and four pesticides, as well as elevated nitrate concentrations, arsenic, radon-222, and uranium (Katz and others, 2007). The construction and operational practices of this PSW are representative of many public-supply wells that use the Upper Floridan aquifer for supplying the population of northern Tampa Bay, which includes Hillsborough, Pinellas, Pasco, and Hernando Counties. In addition, Temple Terrace was willing to make available one of their primary community water-system public-supply wells. The combination of the detected constituents, cooperation of the city utility, and typical well construction and operational practices prompted the selection of this PSW for the local-scale study.

The local-scale study area, which is the focus of this report, is located in west-central peninsular Florida within Temple Terrace, in the northern Tampa Bay region (figs. 1 and 2). The local-scale study area is 86.25 km^2 and is underlain by the Floridan aquifer system. This aquifer system underlies much of the southeastern United States, and its main productive zone, the Upper Floridan aquifer, is a major drinking-water source for nearly 10 million people in Alabama, Florida, Georgia, and South Carolina (Marella and Berndt, 2005), including the Tampa Bay region and Temple Terrace. The local-scale study area is bounded on the west

and southwest by Tampa. The local-scale study area and the local-scale model area are identical in boundary and area. The local-scale study area and model boundary were determined by using the regional-scale model to identify the ACR of the PSW and bounding the likely ACR with the local-scale model area. The model area is oriented to incorporate the primary karst feature orientation, which would minimize error in cell-to-cell flows.

The Upper Floridan aquifer varies from unconfined to confined conditions in the local-scale study area but is mainly classified as unconfined or semiconfined. Numerous karst features are present, including sinkholes and solution-enlarged fractures and bedding plains. About 35 sinkholes were reported in the local-scale study area; however, many more sinkholes probably are present and are buried, filled, or not reported. Several springs are present within or near the local-scale study area (fig. 2). The local-scale study area is oriented around two sharp bends of the Hillsborough River and includes a terraced area that trends from the northwestern study area boundary to the southeast toward the river in the center of the local-scale study area (fig. 3). The local-scale study area also includes floodplains near the river, sinkholes throughout, and deeper sinkholes on the terrace. Most of the land use in the local-scale study area is residential with commercial strips along major roadways (fig. 2). Tributaries include Cypress Creek, which is located in the northern wetlands area, Cow House Creek (figs. 2 and 3). The Tampa Bypass Canal removes water from the Upper Floridan aquifer.

Climate

The climate in the northern Tampa Bay region is characterized by warm, wet summers and relatively dry, mild winters, with an average annual temperature for Tampa, Florida, of 22.4 °C (Owenby and Ezell, 1992). Average rainfall for Temple Terrace between 1993 and 2005 (Mike Darrow, City of Temple Terrace, written commun., 2005) was 152.50 cm/yr, but was as low as 101 cm/yr during extreme drought conditions in 2000 and as high as 205 cm/yr during extreme wet conditions in 2004. Rainfall amounts vary seasonally with more than half of the total annual rainfall usually occurring between June and September. The wettest months are usually August and September (average of 23.33 and 23.67 cm, respectively, from 1993 to 2005) with most of the rainfall occurring as afternoon thunderstorms, tropical storms, and hurricanes. On average, this region experiences high evapotranspiration rates of 114 to 150 cm/yr, as occurred during 1962-92 (Owenby and Ezell, 1992), and high recharge of up to 51 cm/yr. Pan evaporation rates average 125 to 150 cm/yr (Farnsworth and others, 1982).

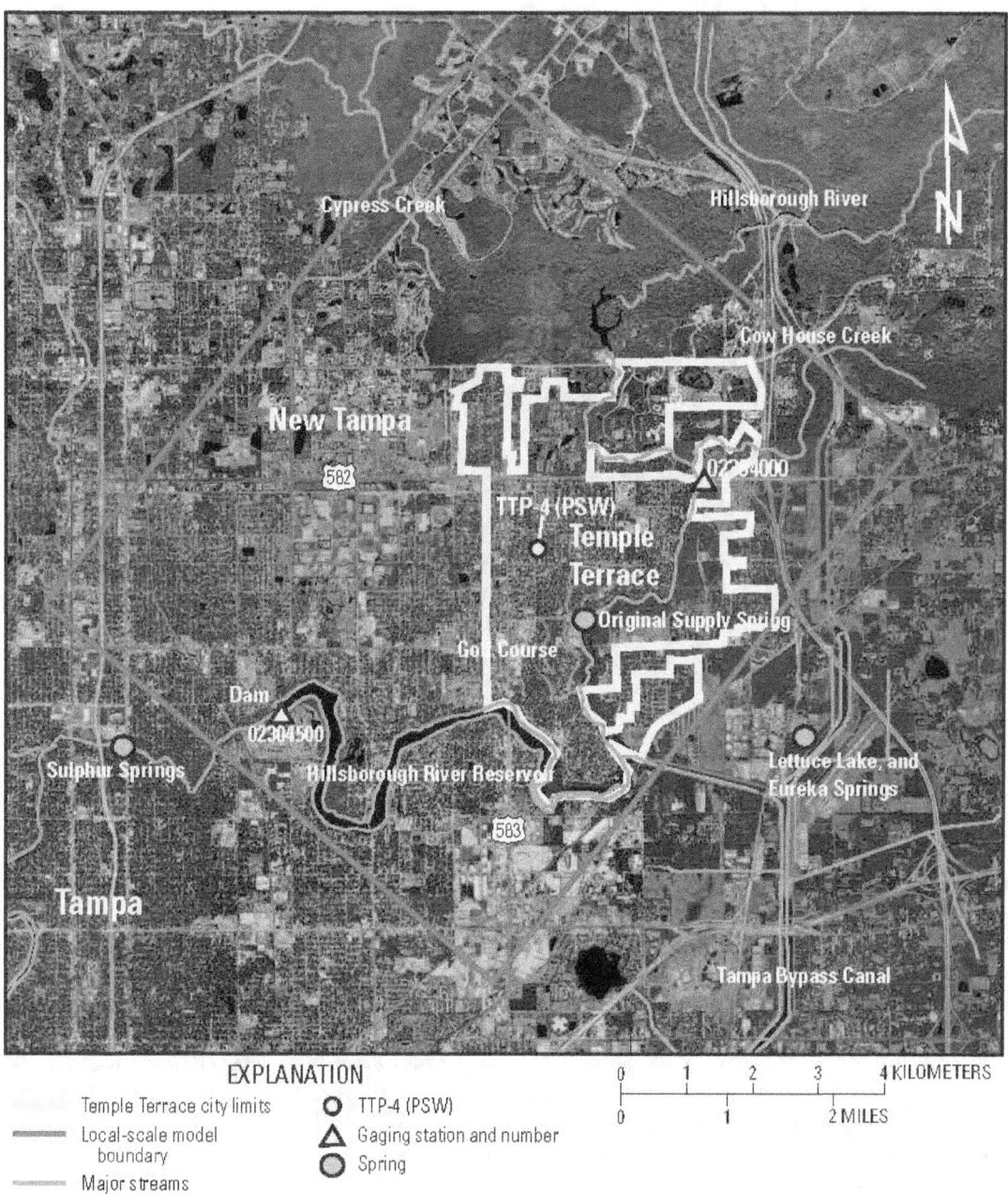

Figure 2. Local-scale study area projected over the digital-orthographic-quarter quadrangle showing City of Temple Terrace boundary, nearby cities, springs, streams, gaging stations, and the selected public-supply well (PSW).

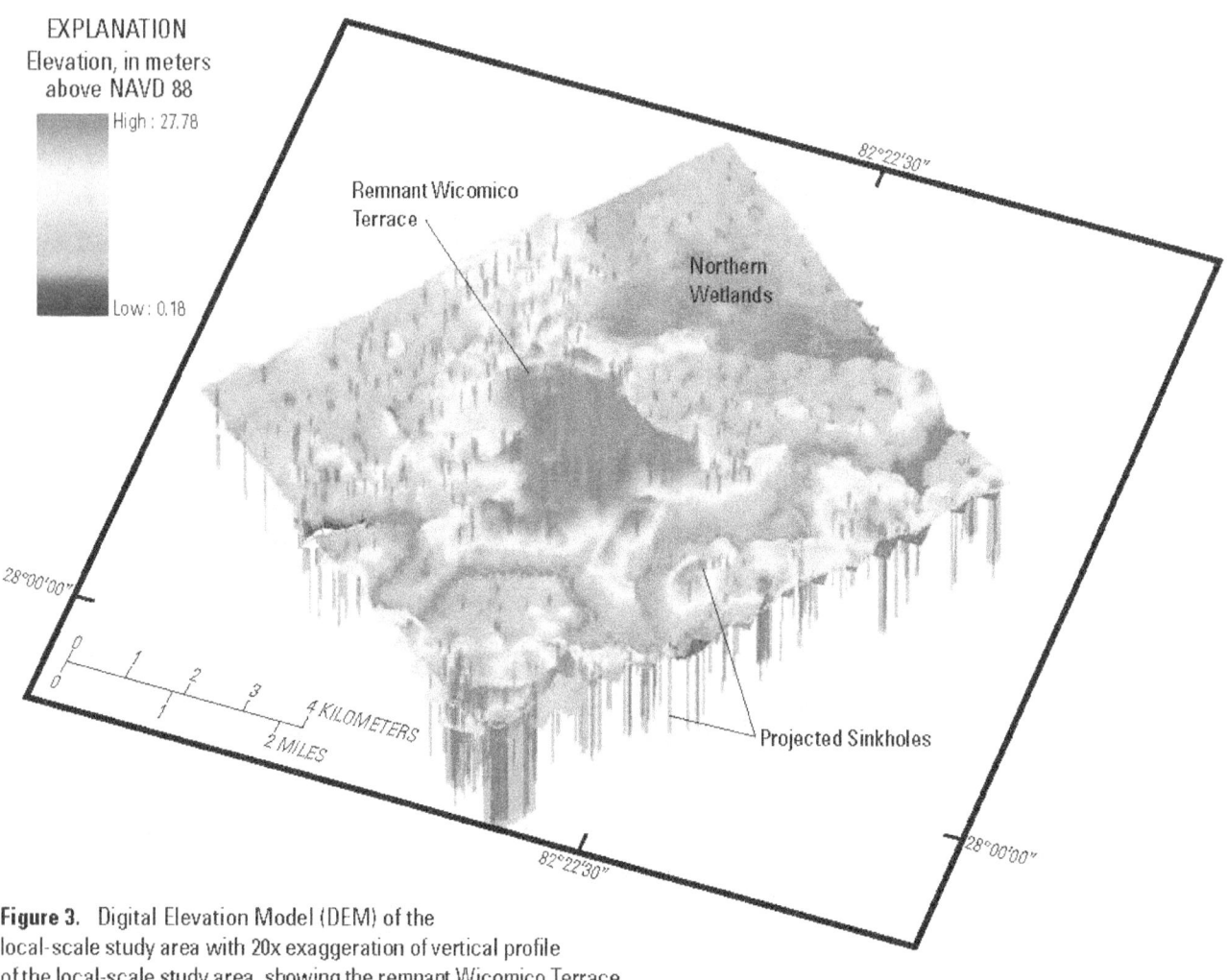

EXPLANATION
Elevation, in meters
above NAVD 88

High : 27.78

Low : 0.18

Remnant Wicomico Terrace

Northern Wetlands

Projected Sinkholes

82°22'30"

28°00'00"

82°22'30"

28°00'00"

0   1   2   3   4 KILOMETERS
0   1   2 MILES

Figure 3.   Digital Elevation Model (DEM) of the local-scale study area with 20x exaggeration of vertical profile of the local-scale study area, showing the remnant Wicomico Terrace, numerous sinkholes projected from the DEM and the Northern Wetlands.

Population and Land Use

Temple Terrace, nested within suburban Tampa, has grown from a small, isolated town of 29 residents in 1920, to 433 residents in 1950, to a city of more than 23,000 residents in 2000 (City of Temple Terrace, 2006). The city was one of the Nation's first planned communities, with parks and a golf course incorporated into the original design of the town. Some citrus groves were still located within the city limits until the 1950s (Stewart and others, 1978); however, the predominant land use changed from primarily citrus agriculture to residential/commercial between 1920 and 1975. Land use has remained relatively stable since that time at about 84 percent urban (mostly residential), 6 percent rangeland, 4 percent wetland, and 4 percent agriculture (Homer and others, 2000). Commercial development has occurred mainly along major corridors. Other major land-use/land-cover features include an 18-hole golf course, which runs parallel to the northeastern

bank of the Hillsborough River, and numerous residential developments built around sinkhole lakes. Paved areas, strip malls, and industrial land uses are also present in the study area.

Physiography

The local-scale study area is located in the coastal lowlands region of the southeastern United States. The coastal lowlands physiographic province consists of a relatively flat plain bounded by an erosional escarpment formed by the remnant Wicomico Terrace (fig. 3; White, 1970). The terrace generally parallels the coast, having been formed by seas that once stood at higher levels than at present. This dominant physiographic feature includes a sandy ridge on which lies much of the City of Temple Terrace. Land-surface elevation ranges from 24.4 m on the western side of the terrace, to 27.4 m along the central part of the terrace (Stewart and others, 1978), and decreases to less than 6 m near the river; average elevation is about 15 m. Other dominant physiographic features in the local-scale study area include the Hillsborough River floodplain, which is deeply incised (3-6 m) in the valley (Stewart and others, 1978). Sinkholes as deep as 6 to 8 are also common in the local-scale study area (fig. 3; Trommer, 1987), and many have been filled and used for stormwater retention ponds. Sandy soils that cover the local-scale study area are well drained and have relatively deep water tables, rapid percolation, internal drainage, and high recharge potential (HydroGeoLogic, Inc., 1997).

Surface-Water and Groundwater Interactions

The Hillsborough River meanders through the local-scale study area, from the northeastern to the southwestern boundaries, and discharges to Hillsborough Bay (a part of the greater Tampa Bay) about 16 km downstream from the local-scale study area (figs. 1 and 2). Much of the channel is defined and controlled by karst features (Lewelling, 2004). Average annual flow was recorded to be 12.8 m³/s between 1939 and September 2000, the period of record (Coffin and Fletcher, 2001). Natural flow in the Hillsborough River was disrupted in the 1920s when a hydroelectric dam was installed near the southwestern edge of the local-scale study area. The Hillsborough River and its tributaries, Cow House Creek and Cypress Creek (fig. 2) in the Temple Terrace area, are affected by backwater from the Hillsborough River Reservoir (Fernandez and others, 1984) so that flow to and from the river is largely controlled by reservoir stage.

The Hillsborough River is in direct hydraulic contact with the surficial aquifer system and the Upper Floridan aquifer in the local-scale study area. The river usually gains water from groundwater discharge as it meanders through the northern part of the local-scale study area; however, some gains in surface water through upward leakage may be lost to evapotranspiration, especially in the northern wetlands (Goetz and others, 1978). Below the Fowler Avenue gaging station (station number 02304000 in fig. 2), the Hillsborough River occasionally loses water to the Upper Floridan aquifer during high-flow events (Wolansky and Thompson, 1987).

Hydrogeologic Setting

The local-scale study area is underlain by three primary hydrogeologic units that include the surficial aquifer system, intermediate confining unit, and Floridan aquifer system; the local- and regional-scale studies primarily include the Upper Floridan aquifer (fig. 4). The Lower Floridan aquifer is present in the regional-scale study area, but is separated from the Upper Floridan aquifer by a middle confining unit; the Lower Floridan aquifer is not present in the local-scale study area (Miller, 1986).

Each hydrogeologic unit is defined by specific geologic units that give each unique hydraulic and hydrogeologic characteristics and guide groundwater flow model layer design.

Geology

The local-scale study area is underlain by sand, clayey sand, sandy clay, clay, and carbonate rocks that were deposited in primarily marine environments during the middle and late Eocene to Holocene ages of the Tertiary Period of the Cenozoic Era. During this time, changes in sea level produced terraces and marine environments in areas that are dry land today. The geologic framework is characterized by multiple layers of sand to clayey sand to sandy clay to clay that overlie a highly weathered thick limestone sequence containing numerous dissolution (karst) features. Numerous localized surface or buried depressions (collapse features or sinkholes) disrupt the layered horizontal geologic framework and form vertical conduit features in layers where dissolution has occurred. In addition, dissolution features occur along the bedding plain and bedding-plain fractures that also add to the karst character of the Upper Floridan aquifer. Fractures are bimodal along two major axes of orientation with the most common orientation at about 310° and the second most common at 40°. The fracture orientations are approximately parallel and perpendicular to the major structural element (Ocala Platform) of the Florida Peninsula in the regional- and local-scale study areas (Schmidt, 1994). Numerous springs are present in the streambed of the Hillsborough River directly outside the local-scale study area (fig. 2).

Lithology

The lithology of the surficial sediments, clay unit, and limestone that compose the hydrogeologic units (surficial aquifer system, intermediate confining unit, and Upper Floridan aquifer, respectively) were described based on analysis of well cuttings, split-spoon coring, and grain-size analysis (Katz and others, 2007). Mineralogical analyses of selected cores were also performed using x-ray diffraction and mass spectrometery. Details about the lithology, depth of saturation, and results of the grain-size analysis for selected wells are presented in Katz and others (2007) and are summarized in the following paragraphs.

The uppermost surficial sediments are a well sorted, very fine to fine quartz sand of Holocene age, and generally less than 3 m thick (95 percent). The remaining surficial sediment consists of silts and clays with thicknesses that range from about 6 to 15 m thick. Surficial sediments are thinnest on the eastern boundary of the local-scale study area near the Hillsborough River, and thickest in the middle and along the western edge of the local-scale study area where sand terraces are present. The sand is white to buff colored near the surface and contains a mixture of organic matter and silt. Below the organic layer, the sand is stained a pale-yellow-orange color,

SERIES	STRATIGRAPHIC UNIT	GENERAL LITHOLOGY	HYDROGEOLOGIC UNIT	MODEL LAYER
Holocene to Pliocene	Undifferentiated Sands and Clays	**Quartz sand**, silty sand, clayey sand, peat, shell	Surficial aquifer system	Layers 1-3
Holocene to Pliocene	Hawthorn Group	**Clay**, minor quartz sand, phosphate, fine-grained dolomite, residual limestone	Intermediate confining unit	Layer 4
Miocene	Hawthorn Group: Tampa Member of the Arcadia Formation	**Limestone**, minor quartz sand, phosphate, chert, clay, fine-grained dolomite	Upper Floridan aquifer: Tampa/Suwannee producing zone	Layers 5-7 Layer 8 Layers 9-11
Oligocene	Suwannee Limestone	**Limestone**, packstone to grainstone, trace quartz sand, organics, variable dolomite and clay content, highly fossiliferous, vuggy	Upper Floridan aquifer: Tampa/Suwannee producing zone	Layers 9-11 Layer 12
Eocene	Ocala Limestone	**Limestone**, micritic, chalky, very fine to fine-grained, soft, poorly indurated, trace organics, clays and dolomite, abundant foraminifera	Upper Floridan aquifer: Ocala semiconfining unit Ocala/Avon Park producing zone	Layer 12 Layer 13
Eocene	Avon Park Formation	**Limestone, dolomite, and evaporites**; Limestone and dolomite interbeds typical in upper part, deeper beds are continuous dolomite with increasing evaporites at base **Limestone** is fine-grained, tan, recrystallized packstone with variable amounts of organic-rich laminations near top **Dolomite** is hard, brown, sucrosic in texture and commonly fractured **Evaporites** occur in dolomite as interstitial gypsum and anhydrite with evaporite filling pore space and as interbeds in the lower part	Upper Floridan aquifer: Avon Park producing zone Middle confining unit	Layer 13 Below the freshwater production zone

Figure 4. Geologic and hydrogeologic stratigraphic column.

which is probably due to the influence of iron leaching into the shallow groundwater system. The clay content gradually increases, creating a sequence of clayey sand generally less than 1 m thick. The sand content ranges from 52 to 95 percent, and the remaining sediment is composed of silt and clay. The clayey sand sequence is the most variable in terms of mineralogy, which probably is due to the variability in the clay content.

Below the clayey sand sequence, the clay content increases, grading to a sequence of sandy clay of the Hawthorn Group of late Miocene age, which corresponds to the intermediate confining unit. The intermediate confining unit in the local-scale study area varies in clay content, consistency, color, composition, and permeability. Generally, the unit has a dense plastic consistency, is tan or greenish-gray or orange-red, and contains varying amounts of sand, chert, and carbonate mud. The clay may be calcareous in places, particularly near the underlying limestone contact. Thickness ranges from 0 to less than 2 m in the local-scale study area. Carr and Alverson (1959) and Sinclair (1974) describe the clay of the intermediate confining unit as a weathered residuum of the underlying Tampa Member limestone.

The highly weathered limestone of the Tampa Member of the Arcadia Formation of the Hawthorn Group underlies the intermediate confining unit in the local-scale study area and is identified as the top of the Upper Floridan aquifer. The Tampa Member of early Miocene age varies from tan to white, is soft to hard, usually sandy, and fossiliferous; it commonly contains clay lenses and cavities. The Tampa Member is generally less than 30 m thick, based on well cuttings collected from 14 wells throughout the local-scale study area, and the depth of the top of the Tampa Member ranges from 3.5 to 12 m below land surface. For two wells, the sands and clays were found far below the typical depth to limestone, which suggests that infilling of overburden materials into cavities has occurred. This infilling of limestone cavities increases the interconnection of overlying units to the Upper Floridan aquifer. Within the Tampa Member is a horizontally extensive layer containing expansive conduits, fractures, and (or) bedding plain erosional features. This information is based on well logs and the nearly instantaneous drawdown experienced by the selected PSW when other public-supply wells in the area open to this zone are turned on. Also, many conduits were noted in three wells open to this layer: wells PSW, MAS-R-F160, and WP-F150.

The Suwannee Limestone of Oligocene age in the Upper Floridan aquifer underlies the Tampa Member, and its thickness is about 60 to 80 m in the local-scale study area. The limestone is pure calcium carbonate in composition, white to light tan, soft and granular, and contains abundant fossil detritus and organic structures such as casts, molds, and borings of mollusks and tests of foraminifera and bryozoans (Carr and Alverson, 1959). Many fossil molds within this rock unit result in a high porosity.

Below the Suwannee Limestone are the Ocala Limestone of late Eocene age and the Avon Park Formation of early to middle Eocene age (Miller, 1986). Both are part of the Upper Floridan aquifer. The Ocala Limestone is a soft, friable, white coquina composed of fossil foraminifera, echinoid, and bryozoans fragments loosely bound in a micritic cement. This unit is also highly porous and dissolution features are abundant. The Avon Park Formation is another highly fractured, karstic, porous, dolomitic limestone with very high permeability due to the karst features. The freshwater interface, defined as the level of 5,000 mg/L chloride concentration in the Upper Floridan aquifer, occurs in the Avon Park Formation in the local-scale study area. The combined thickness of the Ocala Limestone and Avon Park Formation above the 5,000-mg/L chloride line ranges from 72.5 to 105.0 m with a median of 88.7 m. The entire Upper Floridan aquifer freshwater flow system lies above the middle confining unit. The freshwater/saltwater interface is a no-flow boundary (Reilly, 2001). Only the freshwater part of the flow system is discussed in this report.

Groundwater Flow System

The potentiometric surface of the surficial aquifer system generally follows land-surface elevations and is mostly saturated in areas where land elevations are low and not present on the terraces. The depth to the water table is variable and ranges from about 3 to 16 m below land surface. The surficial aquifer system is recharged primarily by the infiltration of rainfall. Recharge is relatively rapid because of the highly permeable surficial sands. The surficial aquifer system is not used as a source of water supply in the study area because of the relatively low yields to wells of less than 19 L/min.

Because of its low permeability, the intermediate confining unit retards the downward leakage between the surficial aquifer system and Upper Floridan aquifer. The occurrence, thickness, and permeability of this unit are highly variable throughout the local-scale study area. Breaches form in this unit due to the dissolution and collapse of the underlying limestone of the Upper Floridan aquifer, facilitating preferential pathways for leakage to the Upper Floridan aquifer.

In the Upper Floridan aquifer, most of the production wells in the local-scale study area are open to the Tampa Member or the Suwannee Limestone. Wells that are deeper than about 100 m probably tap the upper part of the Ocala Limestone and (or) Avon Park Formation (Stewart and others, 1978). The total thickness of the active flow system of the Upper Floridan aquifer ranges from 200 to 280 m in the local-scale study area.

Production and monitoring wells in Hillsborough County have open intervals of relatively large diameters, usually greater than 3 m (Stewart and others, 1978). These large diameters intersect solution openings and cavities in most wells. The selected PSW is open to one of these highly productive, cavernous, water-yielding zones in the Tampa Member of the Upper Floridan aquifer. The top of the highly productive cavernous zone is present at about 36 to 55 m below land surface (Stewart and others, 1978). Wells tapping this zone can yield as much as 5,700 L/min.

Groundwater in the study area flows downward and laterally through the surficial aquifer system until it reaches the intermediate confining unit. Water then moves laterally along the contact between the surficial aquifer system and intermediate confining unit until it encounters a surface-water feature (river, stream, or depression) or breaches into the intermediate confining unit. Breaches serve as preferential flow paths for leaking water to the Upper Floridan aquifer and allow water to short circuit slower flow paths through the intermediate confining unit. Water that leaks into the Upper Floridan aquifer may move slowly in the porous matrix or through secondary porosity features, such as conduits. The water then travels rapidly to wells, springs, rivers, streams or to a large regional discharge feature, such as Tampa Bay or the Gulf of Mexico. The conceptual groundwater flow system is presented in figure 5.

The groundwater flow direction in the surficial aquifer system is approximately from the northwest to southeast in the local-scale study area (fig. 6) and reflects land-surface elevation and local discharge features. The potentiometric surface of the surficial aquifer system is generally above the Upper Floridan aquifer, and highest in a well in the west-central part of the local-scale study area on the remnant Wicomico Terrace. The water level in this well also may be affected by water levels in a nearby stormwater retention pond. Generally, water levels in storm retention ponds are far above those of the surficial aquifer system and the Upper Floridan aquifer.

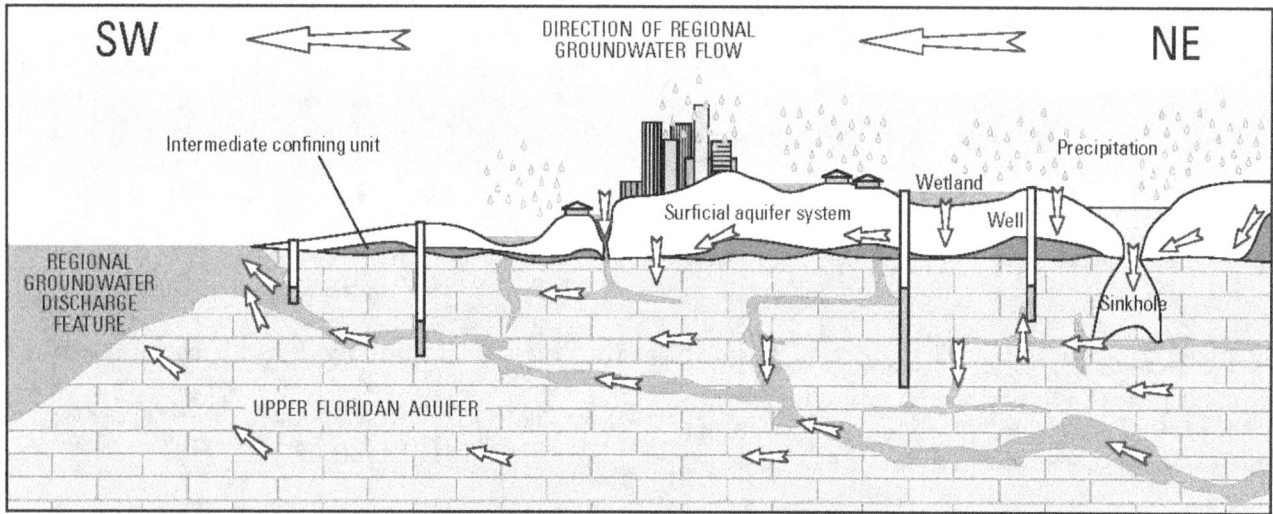

Figure 5. Conceptual diagram of recharge, hydrogeology, and groundwater flow system dynamics for the local-scale study area.

Groundwater flow direction in the Upper Floridan aquifer is also approximately from north to south or southeast in the local-scale study area (fig. 6). Locally, pumping affects hydraulic heads in the Upper Floridan aquifer, most noticeably in the zone that most of Temple Terrace public-supply wells are opened to (the highly transmissive cavernous zone). Pumping of production wells causes local instantaneous drawdown adjacent to production wells. The Upper Floridan aquifer appears to be in direct hydraulic connection with the Hillsborough River. Near the river, the groundwater flow direction depends upon reservoir operations. For example, before a major rainfall event (such as a hurricane), the reservoir water levels are lowered so the groundwater flow direction is toward the river. During drought conditions, the reservoir levels are kept high so that Tampa can continue to draw water for supply; the groundwater flow direction may be away from the river into the aquifer.

Methods

The methods used for this study were consistent with the objectives of the NAWQA/TANC study, which included the use of similar methods in all four local-scale study area investigations. The uses of MODFLOW to simulate groundwater flow, MODPATH to simulate particle tracking, and similar methods of water-quality data collection and analyses provide consistency and comparability for the TANC local-scale study.

Design of Sampling Network and Data Collection and Analysis

A total of 15 wells were installed in 2003-04 in five nests with three wells in each nest oriented along one of the general directions of groundwater flow to the selected PSW based on the regional-scale model. These nests were: Railway Park (RP), Recreation Center at 113th street (113RC), Gillette Recreation Center (GARC), Terrace Hills Center (THC), and Water Plant (WP) (fig. 7; table 1). Most of the nests consisted of one well screened in the surficial aquifer system, one well screened in the top of the Upper Floridan aquifer, and one well screened deeper in the Upper Floridan aquifer. At well nest 113RC, one well was screened in the intermediate confining unit.

During the summer of 2004, an additional 14 monitoring wells were installed, which provided the study with a total of 29 monitoring wells. However, one well was dry, so the final total was reduced to 28 (fig. 7; table 1). The locations of these additional monitoring wells were selected based on updated estimates of the mapped surface expression of the area contributing water to the selected PSW. Three additional well nests were installed, including MAS, Lightfoot Retention Park (LRP), and 62nd Street Retention Pond (62SRP). Two wells were installed at Lynwood Park (LP)—one screened in the surficial aquifer system and the other screened in the intermediate confining unit. Three shallow wells were screened in the surficial aquifer system and installed at Queensway Retention

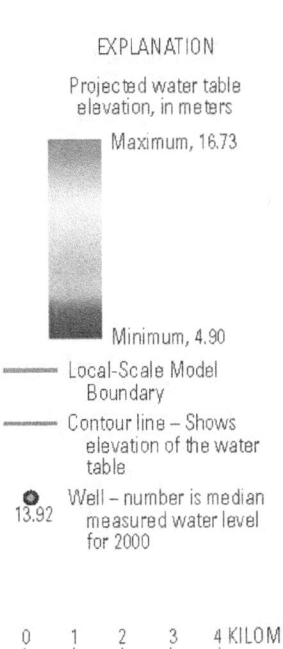

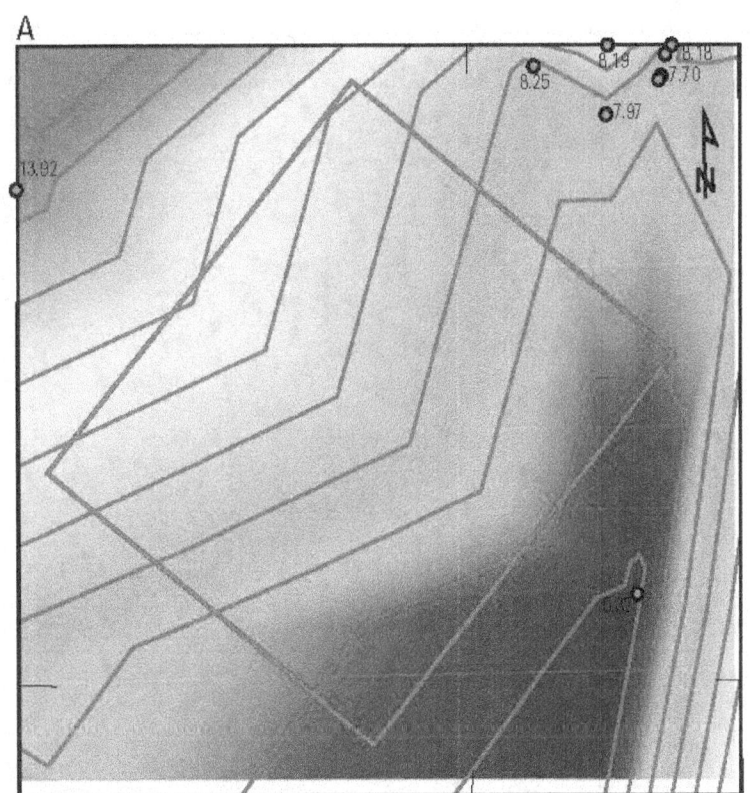

EXPLANATION

Projected water table elevation, in meters

Maximum, 16.73

Minimum, 4.90

Local-Scale Model Boundary

Contour line – Shows elevation of the water table

⊙ Well – number is median
13.92   measured water level for 2000

0   1   2   3   4 KILOMETERS

0   1   2 MILES

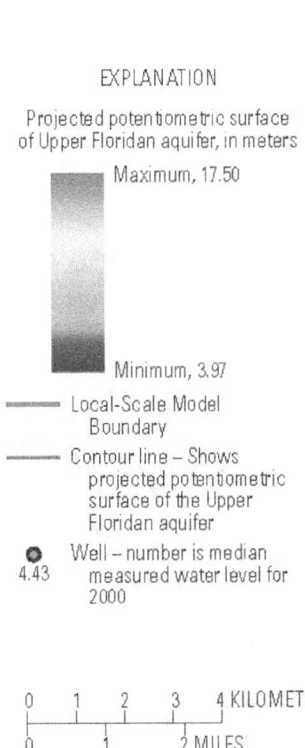

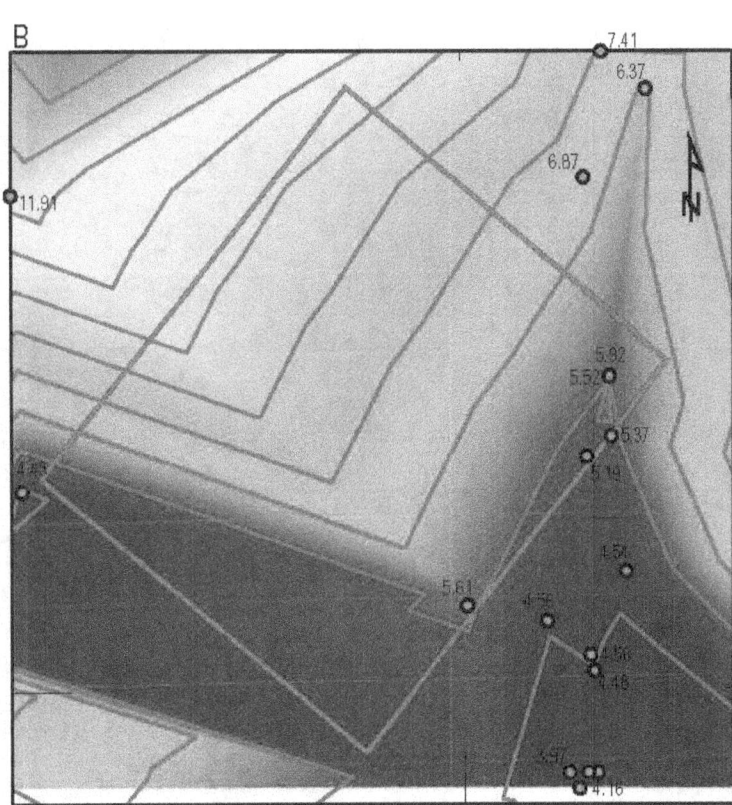

EXPLANATION

Projected potentiometric surface of Upper Floridan aquifer, in meters

Maximum, 17.50

Minimum, 3.97

Local-Scale Model Boundary

Contour line – Shows projected potentiometric surface of the Upper Floridan aquifer

⊙ Well – number is median
4.43   measured water level for 2000

0   1   2   3   4 KILOMETERS

0   1   2 MILES

Figure 6. Median measured water levels and simulated potentiometric surfaces of the (A) surficial aquifer system and (B) Upper Floridan aquifer in the local-scale study area, 2000.

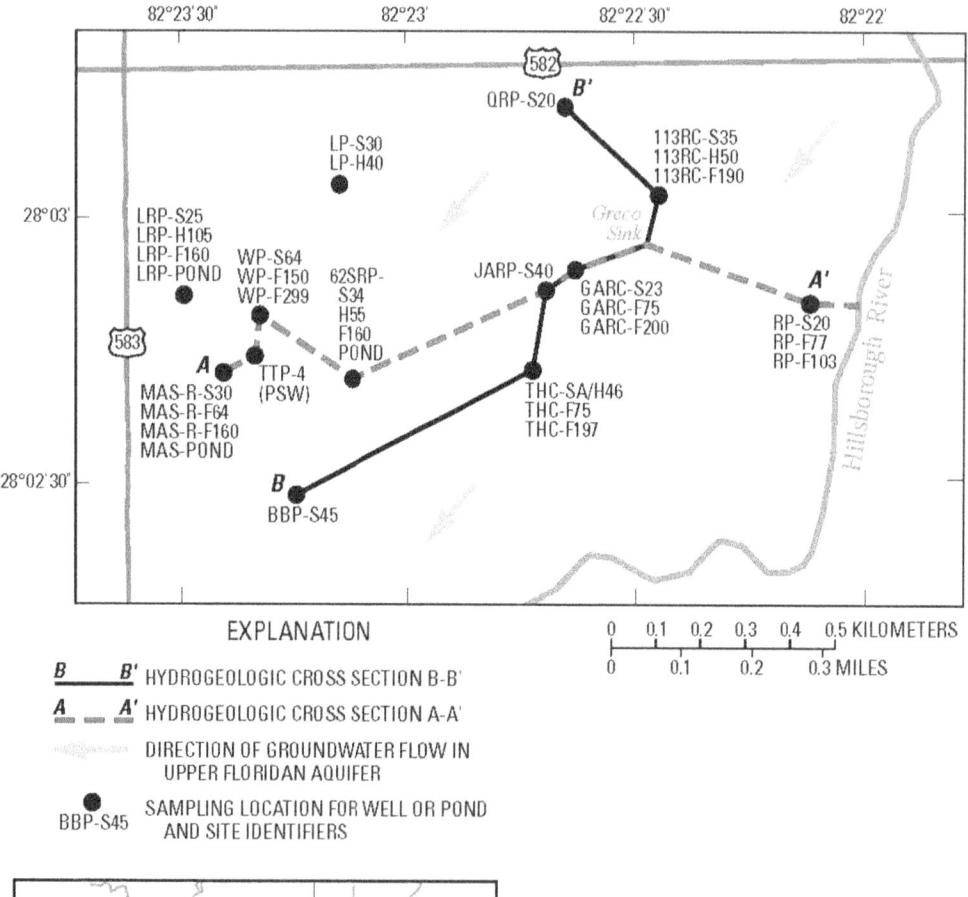

EXPLANATION

B ——— B' HYDROGEOLOGIC CROSS SECTION B-B'

A – – – A' HYDROGEOLOGIC CROSS SECTION A-A'

DIRECTION OF GROUNDWATER FLOW IN
UPPER FLORIDAN AQUIFER

●
BBP-S45 SAMPLING LOCATION FOR WELL OR POND
AND SITE IDENTIFIERS

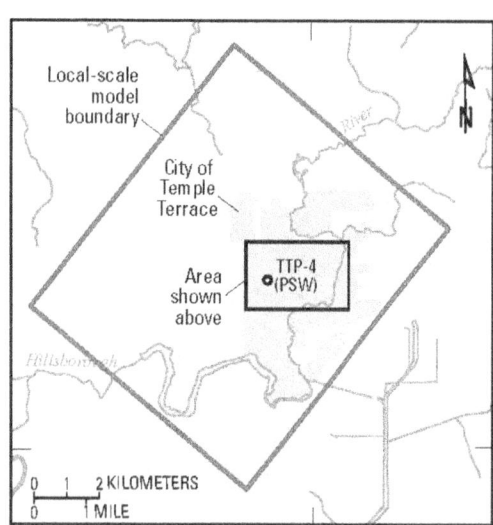

Figure 7. Locations of wells and test holes installed for this study and trace of hydrogeologic sections *A-A'* and *B-B'*. PSW is the selected public-supply well.

Park (QRP), Bonnie Brae Park (BBP), and Jaqueline Arbor (JARP). Surface-water samples were collected from the Hillsborough River (fig. 7) and from stormwater retention ponds at LRP, 62SRP, and MAS (fig. 7). Single wells at the MAS and LRP sites are screened in the intermediate confining unit. Figure 8 presents two hydrogeologic sections through the local-scale study area based on the drillers' logs and core analyses.

Water levels were measured in all monitoring wells during water-quality sampling, and water-level recorders were installed in 14 monitoring wells, 3 retention ponds, and the Hillsborough River at Railway Park to provide water-level data that were used to calibrate the groundwater flow model. Groundwater levels and river stage were recorded hourly from December 2003 until November 2005. The median water-level value, calculated from the hourly groundwater levels or water

Table 1. Inventory of groundwater wells and surface-water sites used in the local-scale study area.

[Well locations shown in fig. 7; NA, not applicable]

Site name	Short site name	Station identifier	Water level recorder	Measuring point altitude, (meters)	Well depth, (meters)
Terrace Hill Circle, Upper Floridan aquifer (lower)	THC-F197	280241082224401	No	15.99	60.05
Terrace Hill Circle, Upper Floridan aquifer (upper)	THC-F75	280241082224402	No	15.91	22.86
Terrace Hill Circle, surficial aquifer system	THC-SA/H46	280241082224403	No	15.83	13.72
Railway Park, Upper Floridan aquifer (lower)	RP-F103	280249082220701	Yes	11.16	31.39
Railway Park, Upper Floridan aquifer (upper)	RP-F77	280249082220702	Yes	11.12	22.86
Railway Park, surficial aquifer system	RP-S20	280249082220703	Yes	11.15	6.1
Railway Park, Hillsborough River	HRIVER	280244082220200	Yes	7.17	NA
Temple Terrace Recreation Center at 113th, Upper Floridan aquifer	113RC-F190	280301082222701	No	12.81	60.96
Temple Terrace Recreation Center at 113th, intermediate confining unit	113RC-H50	280301082222702	No	12.73	15.24
Temple Terrace Recreation Center at 113th, surficial aquifer system	113RC-S35	280301082222703	No	12.8	10.67
Temple Terrace Recreation Center at Gillette, Upper Floridan aquifer (lower)	GARC-F200	280253082223801	Yes	12.42	60.96
Temple Terrace Recreation Center at Gillette, Upper Floridan aquifer (upper)	GARC-F75	280253082223802	No	12.48	22.71
Temple Terrace Recreation Center at Gillette, surficial aquifer system	GARC-S23	280253082223803	Yes	12.23	7.01
Temple Terrace Water Plant, Upper Floridan aquifer (lower)	WP-F299	280247082231901	Yes	24.49	91.44
Temple Terrace Water Plant, Upper Floridan aquifer (upper)	WP-F150	280247082231902	Yes	24.51	45.72
Temple Terrace Water Plant, surficial aquifer system	WP-S64	280247082231903	Yes	24.38	19.81
Temple Terrace City Well No. 4 at Temple Terrace FL	TTP-4 (PSW)	unpublished	No	24.65	53.04
MAS Residence, Upper Floridan aquifer (Lower)	MAS- R-F160	280242082232401	Yes	20.33	48.77
MAS Residence, surficial aquifer system	MAS-R-S30	280242082232403	No	20.31	9.14
MAS Residence, Upper Floridan aquifer (Upper)	MAS-R-F64	280242082232403	Yes	20.34	19.51
MAS Retention Pond	MAS-POND	280242082232900	Yes	15.99	NA
62nd St. Retention Pond, Upper Floridan aquifer (lower)	62SRP-F160	280241082230701	No	21.55	48.77
62nd St. Retention Pond, Upper Floridan aquifer (upper)	62SRP-H55	280241082230702	No	21.67	16.76
62nd St. Retention Pond, surficial aquifer system	62SRP-S34	280241082230703	Yes	21.67	10.36
62nd St. Retention Pond	62SRP-POND	280242082230800	Yes	18.62	NA
Bonnie Brae Park, surficial aquifer system	BBP-S45	280228082231501	Yes	16.22	13.72
Queensway Retention Pond	QRP-S20	280311082223901	No	11	6.1
Jaqueline Arbor Retention Pond surficial well	JARP-S40	280251082224201	No	13.22	11.28
Lynwood Park, Upper Floridan aquifer (upper)	LP-H40	280303082230901	No	15.08	12.5
Lynwood Park, surficial aquifer system	LP-S30	280303082230902	No	15.08	9.14
Lightfoot Recreation Center Retention Pond, Upper Floridan aquifer (lower)	LRP-F160	280250082233001	Yes	20.24	48.77
Lightfoot Recreation Center Retention Pond, Upper Floridan aquifer (upper)	LRP-H105	280250082233002	No	20.28	34.14
Lightfoot Recreation Center Retention Pond, surficial aquifer system	LRP-S25	280250082233003	Yes	20.26	7.62
Lightfoot Recreation Center Retention Pond	LRP-POND	280250082233200	Yes	18.64	NA

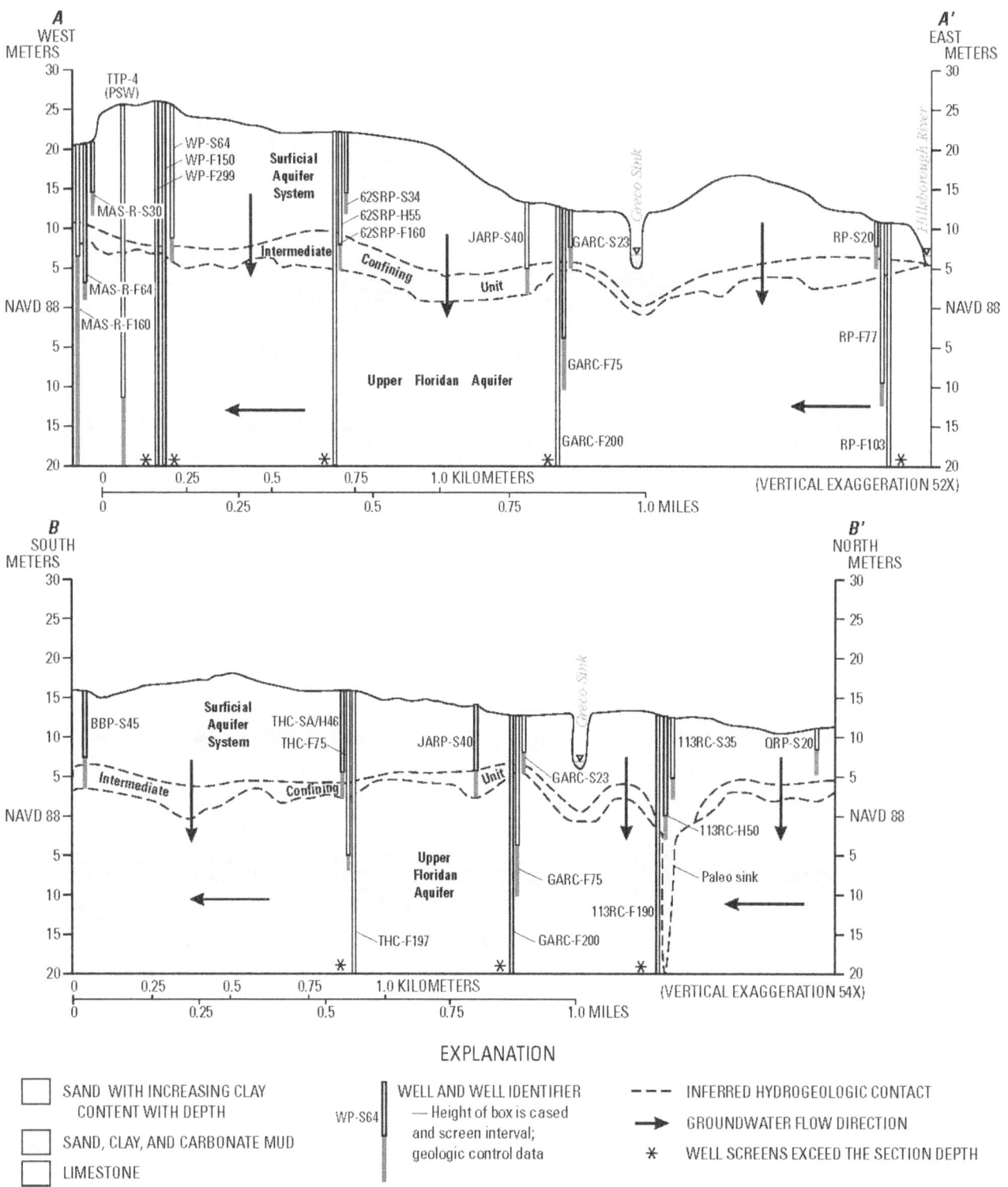

Figure 8. Hydrogeologic sections across the study area. Trace of sections is shown in figure 7. PSW is the selected public-supply well.

levels measured during sampling, was used for comparison to simulated water levels during groundwater flow model calibration. Groundwater levels and retention pond and river-stage data collected for this study are summarized in table 2 and figure 9. Groundwater hydraulic gradients were calculated for measurements for wells open to the surficial aquifer system and intermediate confining unit or Upper Floridan aquifer (if the intermediate confining unit was not present) at well nests GARC, 113RC, RP, THC, and WP, and between the upper and the lower open intervals of the Upper Floridan aquifer at well nests GARC, LRP, MAS, 62SRP, RP, THC, and WP, and used in the parameter estimation process.

Development and Calibration of Local-Scale Groundwater Flow and Particle Tracking Model

A local-scale, steady-state, three-dimensional numerical groundwater flow model was developed and used in this study to evaluate the movement of water and solutes from recharge areas to the selected PSW. The model was nested within the regional model used for the TANC regional analysis (Crandall, 2007). The local-scale model was constructed and run using the USGS finite-difference groundwater flow model MODFLOW 2000 (Harbaugh and others, 2000). The parameter estimation feature of this code was activated to estimate hydraulic parameters and recharge properties using an automated nonlinear-regression approach. Flow paths and traveltimes associated with simulated particles that discharge to wells were determined using MODPATH version 4.3—the USGS particle tracking software (Pollack, 1994). Both the groundwater flow and the particle-tracking simulations were refined in concert to obtain the best match for simulated water levels and groundwater age tracer concentrations and to assure that hydraulic parameter estimates were reasonable. Later, the model was put into UCODE (Poeter and others, 2005), which was used to refine the estimated hydraulic property values from MODFLOW-2000 as well as to estimate porosity values used by MODPATH. The UCODE_2005 is a parameter-estimation program that can be used with any program or combination of programs with numerical (ASCII or text only) input and output files. This program allowed for observations of water-level gradient and concentrations of the environmental tracers, tritium and sulfur hexafluoride, to be used in addition to water levels in estimating the parameters for MODFLOW and MODPATH.

Table 2. Summary of hourly water-level measurements obtained from monitoring wells, stormwater retention ponds, and the Hillsborough River in the local-study area, December 11, 2003 to November 17, 2005.

Short site name	Dates of measurement		Number of days	Water-level measurements, in meters			
	Start date	End date		Mean	Median	Maximum	Minimum
BBP-S45	1/21/2005	11/14/2005	297	6.50	6.43	7.20	5.83
GARC-F200	1/28/2004	11/16/2005	659	6.76	6.62	8.44	5.76
GARC-S23	1/28/2004	11/16/2005	659	6.80	6.62	8.77	5.79
LRP-F160	1/21/2005	11/14/2005	298	6.48	6.41	7.11	5.82
LRP-POND	5/26/2005	11/7/2005	166	18.66	18.66	19.19	18.43
LRP-S25	1/21/2005	11/14/2005	297	17.32	17.26	18.03	16.66
62SRP-S34	6/10/2005	10/24/2005	135	12.64	12.74	13.12	11.96
62SRP-POND	5/31/2005	11/2/2005	112	18.27	18.27	19.67	17.61
HRIVER	12/12/2003	11/16/2005	704	6.58	6.62	7.07	5.90
MAS-R-F160	1/21/2005	11/14/2005	297	6.48	6.43	7.14	5.86
MAS-R-F64	1/21/2005	11/14/2005	296	7.17	7.00	7.97	6.66
MAS-POND	5/25/2005	11/14/2005	174	15.67	15.64	17.90	14.83
RP-F103	12/11/2003	11/17/2005	689	6.64	6.57	7.84	5.77
RP-F77	12/11/2003	11/17/2005	708	6.66	6.56	8.00	5.79
RP-S20	12/11/2003	11/17/2005	640	6.87	6.73	8.22	6.01
WP-F150	12/11/2003	11/16/2005	685	6.45	6.35	7.85	5.50
WP-F299	12/11/2003	11/16/2005	639	6.34	6.27	7.43	5.55
WP-S64	12/11/2003	11/16/2005	639	8.56	8.37	10.10	8.13

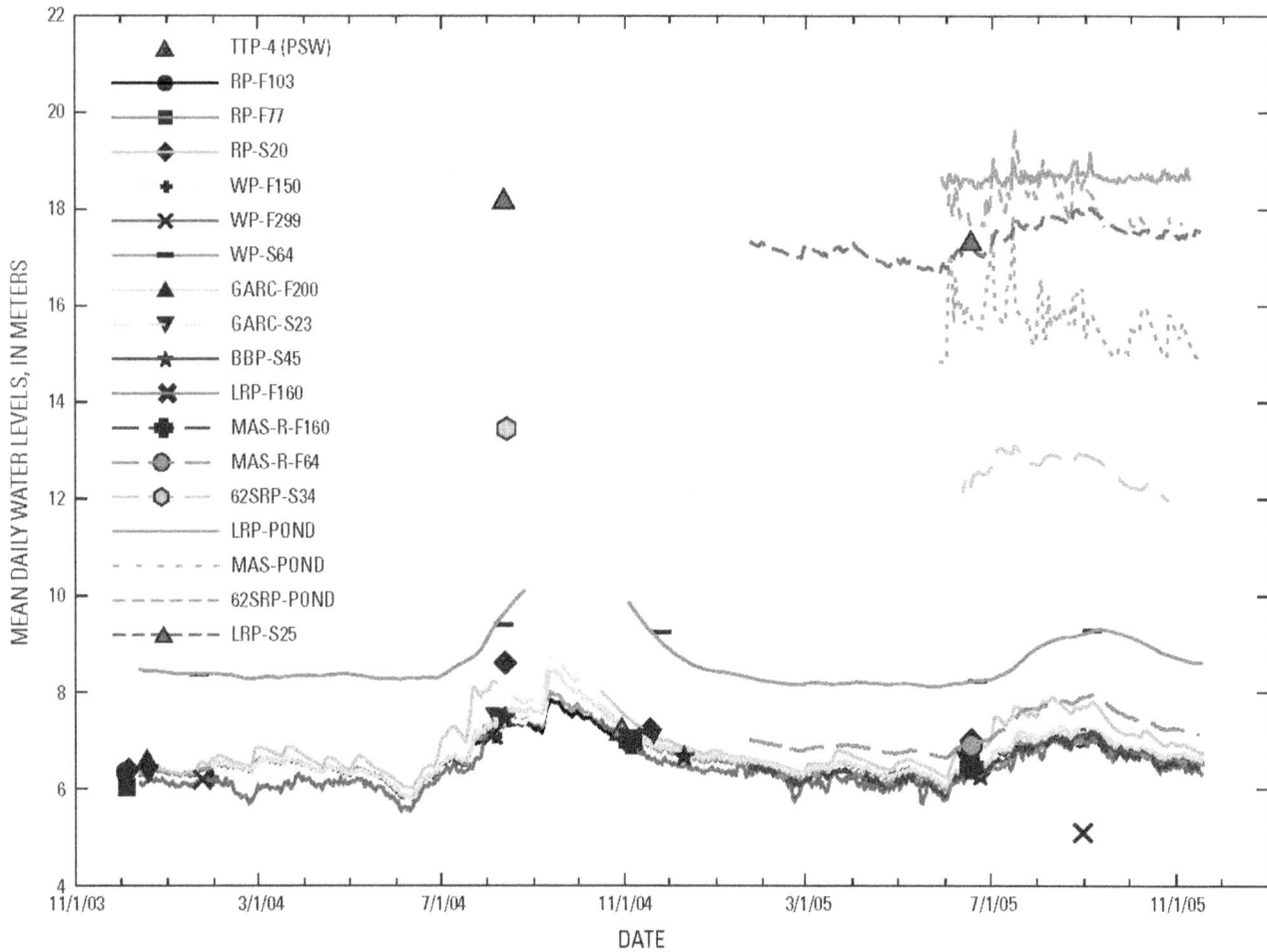

Figure 9. Median daily water levels from continuous water-level recorders in monitoring wells, stormwater retention ponds, and the Hillsborough River station, and various isolated measurements made in the local-scale study area, December 11, 2003 to November 17, 2005. PSW is the selected public-supply well.

Groundwater Flow and Advective Tracking Simulation

The local-scale groundwater flow model simulates steady-state conditions in an aquifer system that is representative of long-term stresses, such as pumping and recharge. Pumping stresses used in the local-scale model are those from calendar year 2000. Pumping during calendar year 2000 was generally representative of pumping that has occurred in the area for the past 15 years or more, and pumping levels are unlikely to change significantly in the foreseeable future, because the area is already fully developed for residential and commercial uses. Also, concerns over declines in lake levels that began in the early 1990s, have prevented further pumping of the Upper Floridan aquifer for water supply. River stages are averages based on long-term gaging station data and regression between

gages. Total recharge in the local-scale model area was based on parameter estimation but was checked against long-term estimates of recharge, which ranged from 12 to 65 cm/yr. The average total recharge in the model area is 33.8 cm/yr. Water levels used for comparison to model output are based on median water levels measured in the 28 wells installed for the TANC local-scale study from 2003 to 2005 and 12 wells operated by Temple Terrace and the Southwest Florida Water Management District.

Model Uncertainties and Limitations

The accuracy of the groundwater flow models is limited by the modeling software, assumptions made during model development, and results of model calibration and sensitivity analysis. A groundwater flow model is a means of portraying and testing a conceptual understanding of an aquifer system.

Because groundwater flow systems are inherently complex, simplifying assumptions are necessary in developing and applying these model codes (Anderson and Woessner, 1992). Groundwater flow models solve for average conditions within each cell. The parameters were interpolated or extrapolated from measurements and (or) estimated during calibration. As such, the intent in developing the groundwater flow model was not to reproduce every detail of the natural system, but rather to portray its dominant characteristics. This is especially true in aquifers with karst features where there is an extreme difference in aquifer properties at scales much smaller than the minimum representation in the numerical model.

Results from the local-scale model described herein should be interpreted generally and are best suited for comparative analysis at this location. However, the model can be used to calculate nitrate concentrations based on particle tracking and this can be used to indicate, in general terms, whether concentrations are likely to go up or down in the selected PSW.

It is assumed for a steady-state model that the system is in equilibrium. Although water-level hydrographs suggest this generally is the case in the local-scale model area over time, the data are not unequivocal. Errors related to this assumption could be notable, and consideration should be taken in interpreting model results and analyses that depend on model output, including particle tracking. The boundary conditions for the local-scale model are derived from the regional-scale model. To the extent that the regional model may contain errors in representing the flow system in the local-scale model domain, the boundary conditions used in the local-scale model also could be a source of model error.

Model Geometry and Discretization

The regional-scale model was used to provide boundary conditions, initial hydraulic heads, initial recharge estimates, drain locations, initial drain and river conductances, and pumping data for the local-scale model. Specified fluxes at the edges of the local-scale model were extracted from the regional model using methods developed by Leake and Claar (1999). The regional model is discussed by Crandall (2007), and updates are presented in the appendix of this report. The regional-scale groundwater flow model calibrated for the regional TANC study covers more than 5,400 km² in the northern Tampa Bay region and consists of 4 layers, 227 columns, and 234 rows with the cell size ranging from 200 to 1,600 m on a side (fig. 10). The regional-scale model was updated using parameter estimation in MODFLOW-2000 to gain better insight into recharge, to determine the most probable flow paths, and to improve estimates of boundary conditions and initial hydraulic properties. These updated hydraulic properties and recharge estimates were used for initial estimates in the local-scale model.

The local-scale model grid has a finer discretization than the regional-scale model and incorporates refined parameter zones and karst features. Hydraulic properties used in the updated regional-scale model were revised during local-scale model calibration. Like the regional-scale model, the local-scale groundwater flow model grid is also rotated 50° counterclockwise from the north to simulate the anisotropy created by the secondary porosity features (the orientation of fracture planes) and to minimize flux errors along primary flow paths. Regionally, the predominant fracture orientation, identified using photolineament techniques by Williams (1985) and Culbreath (1988), is bimodally distributed with maxima at -50 and +40°.

The local-scale model grid is discretized into 5,520 cells (80 rows and 69 columns) of 125 m on each cell side. The local-scale model has 13 layers representing 6 hydrogeologic units (fig. 4). Some model layers may represent the same hydrogeologic unit; for example, model layers 5 to 7 explicitly represent the upper part of the Tampa Member above the conduit layer. The upper and lower parts of the Tampa Member hydrogeologic unit was subdivided into multiple model layers for geochemical or particle tracking purposes to prevent problems with weak sinks. In these cases, the properties of the hydrogeologic unit remain unchanged throughout the multiple layers composing the unit.

Model layers 1 to 3 correspond to the surficial aquifer system (fig. 4). The top of this layer ranges from 0.83 to 26.23 m above NAVD 1988; the bottom ranges from 0.83 to 6.42 m above NAVD 1988. The thickness of this unit generally ranges from 0 to 21.78 m, but can be much greater where sinkholes are present because of surficial materials that collapse into the solution features. The median thickness of the three layers composing the surficial aquifer system is 5.36 m. This hydrogeologic unit was divided into three model layers to attempt to track changes in oxidation-reduction processes encountered along flow paths. Layer 1 is active predominately on the terraces and is inactive in the northern part of the model area in and along the Hillsborough River. Layer 2 is active in 87 percent of the model-grid cells and is inactive in or along the Hillsborough River on the eastern side of the model area and along the westernmost Hillsborough River cells below the dam, along Cow House Creek, in drain cells on the western edge of the model area, and in the northern wetlands. Layer 3 is active throughout most of the model area and is inactive in river cells below the dam and drain cells on the southeastern part of the model area. The three layers that correspond to the surficial aquifer system have identical hydraulic properties.

Layer 4 represents the intermediate confining unit. The bottom of this layer ranges from -0.48 m below to 5.42 m above NAVD 1988, and the median is 2.73 m above NAVD 1988. The areal extent of layer 4 is identical to that described for model layer 3. The thickness of layer 4 is set to 1 m throughout the model area because, in some areas, the layer is either not present or very thin, which causes problems for solving the matrix. Layer 4 hydraulic properties alternate

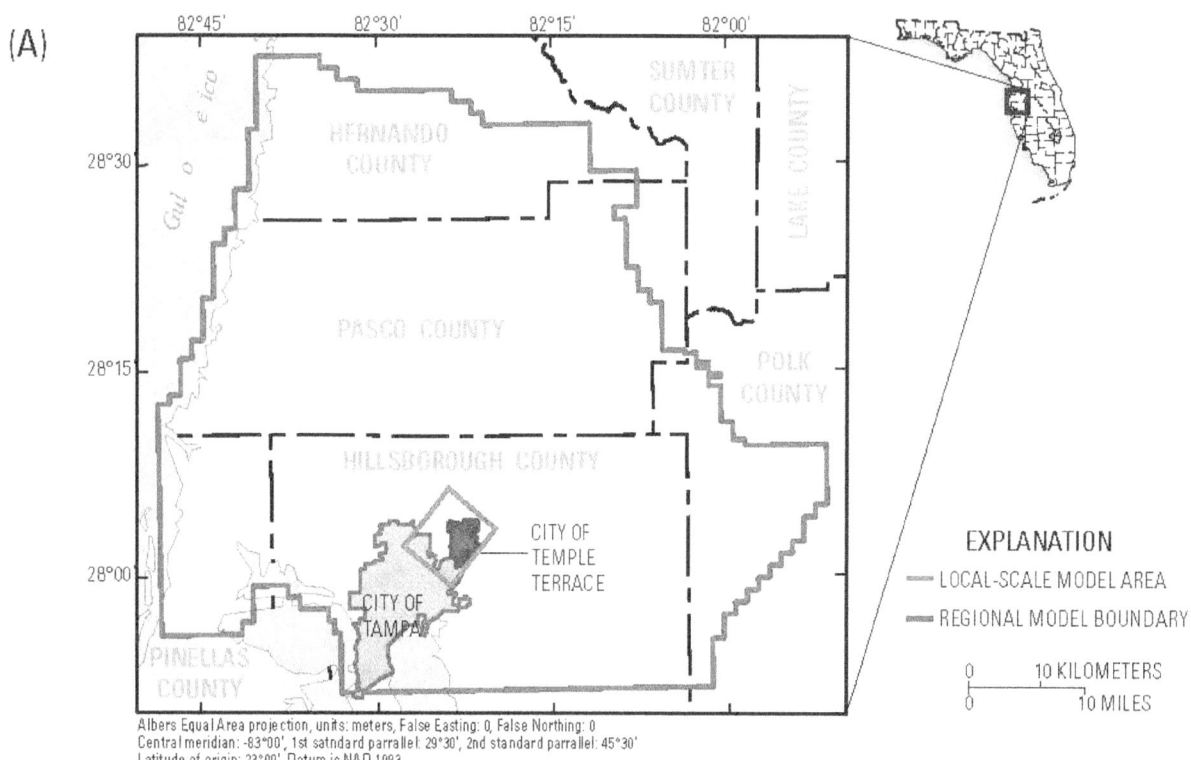

(A)

Albers Equal Area projection, units: meters, False Easting: 0, False Northing: 0
Central meridian: -83°00', 1st satndard parrallel: 29°30', 2nd standard parrallel: 45°30'
Latitude of origin: 23°00', Datum is NAD 1983

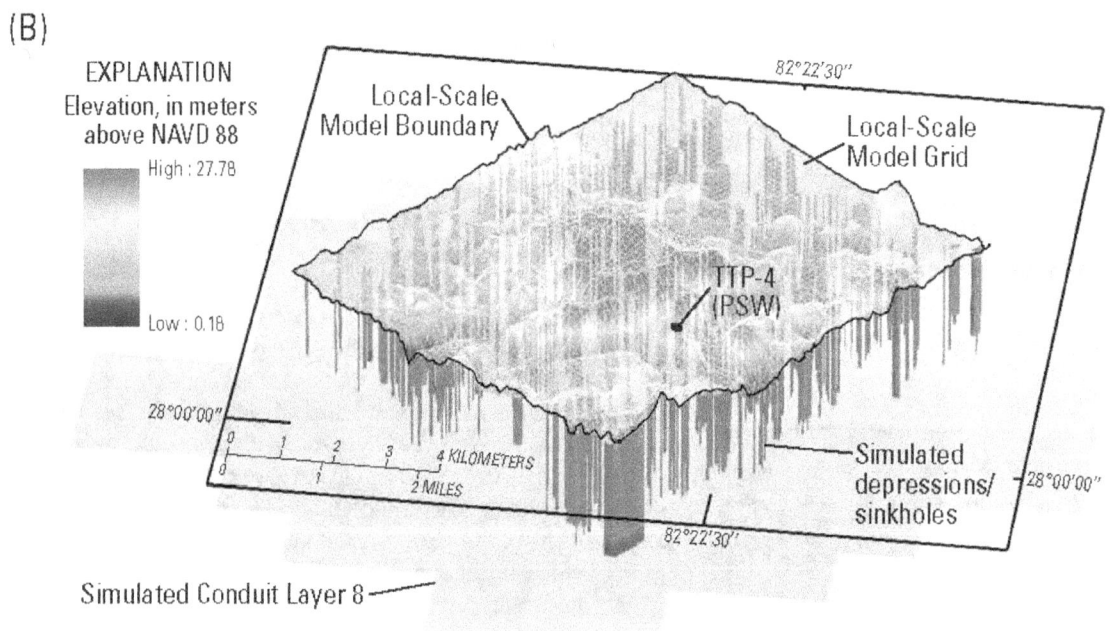

(B)

Figure 10. Local-scale model area in relation to the regional-scale modeled area. PSW is the selected public-supply well.

between those of the surficial aquifer system and intermediate confining unit, depending on whether or not a depression (sinkhole) has been identified in the particular model-grid cell.

Model layers 5 to 11 represent the Tampa Member in the Upper Floridan aquifer. For particle tracking purposes, this unit was subdivided into seven model layers to facilitate geochemical and flow path analysis. Layers 5, 6, and 7 represent the upper part of the Tampa Member and have identical hydraulic properties and thicknesses in corresponding model cells. The bottom of model layer 7 ranges from -18.26 to -29.72 m below NAVD 1988. The median total thickness of layers 5 to 7 is 28.11 m; however, the overall thickness ranges from 21.9 to 34.6 m. Layers 5, 6, and 7 thicken to the south within the Tampa Member. Model layer 8 represents the highly transmissive cavernous zone in the approximate middle of the Tampa Member. This layer was set to a constant thickness of 3 m throughout the model—approximately based on caliper and video logs of the selected PSW. The bottom of layer 8 ranges from -21.3 to -32.7 m below NAVD 1988. Layers 9, 10, and 11 represent the lower part of the Tampa Member. The bottom of layers 9 to 11 ranges from -49.4 to -66.7 m below NAVD 1988. These three layers have identical hydraulic properties and thicknesses for each corresponding row/column address. The median total thickness of model layers 9 to 11 is 34.1 m, but thicknesses range from 28.2 to 36.4 m.

Model layers 12 and 13 represent the Suwannee Limestone and (or) Ocala Limestone and possibly the Avon Park Formation in some places. The lower model boundary coincides with the 5,000-mg/L chloride concentration level. The lower extent of the freshwater flow system (Sepulveda, 2002) at which the chloride boundary occurs ranges from -208.8 to -268.9 m below NAVD 1988. The total thickness of model layers 12 and 13 ranges from 145.1 to 210.0 m with a median thickness of 177.5 m. These model layers thin to the southwest.

Karst features are incorporated into model layers 1 to 11 by using large vertical hydraulic properties, anisotropy, high recharge, and low porosity values where karst features are thought to be present. Locations and diameters of closed-basin depressions (sinkholes) were estimated by compiling available coverages of sinkholes and identifying closed-basin depressions from the digital elevation map. A total of 635 closed-basin depressions were identified in the local-scale model area. Preferential groundwater flow direction due to fracture orientation is simulated in the model by specifying anisotropy, which has the effect of decreasing the value of the hydraulic conductivity by using a multiplication factor between 0 and 1.0 along column cell faces of the model grid for layers 5 to 13 compared to that along row cell faces. Vertical anisotropy was also used in layers 1 to 3 to represent disruption of horizontally deposited layers and flow paths due to collapse features (sinkholes). The karstic nature of layer 8 was simulated in the local-scale model by using large values for the hydraulic properties and low values for the porosity of this layer. Little information exists for the model area about karst features below layer 8.

Boundary Conditions and Model Stresses

Boundary conditions for the local-scale model include specified fluxes entering or exiting the model area at the boundaries, and stresses include recharge from precipitation, discharge from pumping, leakage to or from rivers, and discharge to drains. In the local-scale model, specified fluxes are used for boundary conditions on all sides and layers of the model, except layers 1, 2, and 4. Water flowing across the boundary into these layers is assumed to be negligible.

Description of Lateral Boundaries

The local-scale model employs lateral non-zero fluxes across boundaries so that they do not have to extend to the natural hydrologic groundwater divides, thus allowing the focus of the modeling effort to remain on the ACR of the selected PSW. Specified non-zero flux boundaries are used on all sides of the model area for layers 3 to 13, except in layers 1, 2, and 4. Layers 1 and 2 are not present on all boundaries, so all of the non-zero boundary flux to the surficial aquifer system layers was placed in layer 3. Layer 4 represents the thin, laterally and vertically discontinuous, low permeability, high clay content intermediate confining unit and is most likely incapable of significant fluxes across the model boundaries; therefore, a zero specified-flux boundary condition was imposed on the boundaries for this layer. All specified non-zero boundary fluxes were obtained from the updated regional model and translated to the local-scale model-grid cells.

Flow from the specified flux boundaries enters the model area primarily through the northwestern and northeastern boundaries and discharges from the model area primarily through the southeastern and southwestern boundaries. An appreciable amount of boundary flow entering and discharging from the model area is the result of the low hydraulic heads associated with drains near the southwestern corner of the model grid. The influx to the model area across lateral boundaries (table 3) was 24,297.15 m^3/d (row 1—northeastern boundary) and 16,470.97 m^3/d (column 1—northwestern boundary). Most of the water enters through model layers 8, 12, and 13, and discharges from the local-scale model area through the southeastern (column 69) and southwestern (row 80) boundaries at -20,290.85 and -8,722.76 m^3/d, respectively. Most of the water enters and exits the aquifer through layer 12 at inflows of 17,083.69 m^3/d, and layer 13 at inflows of 11,535.8 m^3/d in the lower part of the model flow system. However, 48.8 percent of the water discharging from the model area flows through layers 5 to 11, representing the upper part of the Upper Floridan aquifer in the Tampa Member. Net discharge occurs from layer 3 through the northeastern and northwestern boundaries in the local-scale model area. The net discharge, although small compared to other boundary fluxes, most likely occurs because wetlands, located directly outside of the northern corner of the local-scale model

Table 3. Summary of specified flux by model boundary and layer.

Layer	Specified flux by model boundary, in cubic meters per day			
	Northeast	Southwest	Northwest	Southeast
3	-251.07	-44.32	-654.32	-237.65
5	673.67	-196.33	519.38	-1,221.60
6	673.67	-196.33	519.38	-1,221.60
7	673.67	-196.33	519.38	-1,221.60
8	3,422.51	-864.17	2,473.2	-5,237.04
9	673.67	-196.33	519.38	-1,221.60
10	673.67	-196.33	519.38	-1,221.60
11	673.67	-196.33	519.38	-1,221.60
12	8,347.99	-3,050.53	5,870.34	-3,750.73
13	8,735.70	-3,585.76	5,665.47	-3,735.83
Total:	24,297.15	-8,722.76	16,470.97	-20,290.85

area, are in the regional-scale model and probably affect the potentiometric surface enough to slope it northward in this area and make the net inflow negative for layer 3.

Simulation of Recharge and Discharge

Recharge is simulated by applying it directly to the top face of the highest active grid cell (layers 1 to 5) of the local-scale model area. Simulated recharge from the infiltration of precipitation averages 33.78 cm/yr throughout the model area (total volumetric recharge/total model area); recharge is increased in cells with depressions or sinkholes (fig. 10). Recharge is applied to layers 1 to 5 (fig. 11); although layer 2 (68 percent by volume) and layer 3 (22 percent by volume) receive the most recharge. Recharge is applied to layer 1 (10 percent of volume), mostly on the northwestern terrace. Less than 1 percent of the total recharge is applied to layers 4 and 5, mainly along the river below the dam (layer 5), in the drains on the southeastern corner (layer 5), and near the center of the southeastern boundary (layer 4).

The Hillsborough River and its major tributaries (Cypress Creek, Cow House Creek, and the Tampa Bypass Canal) were simulated by the local-scale model using the MODFLOW River package (fig. 12). A total of 374 river cells were specified in the model grid. All river cells above the dam are set in layer 3, and river cells below the dam are set in layer 5. For each river cell, river stage and bottom elevations are extrapolated between

upstream gaging station 02303330 (outside of the local-scale model area), gaging station 02304000, and gaging station 02304500 (at the dam), using linear interpolation and available observations (figs. 2 and 11). River bottom elevations were set at a constant 3.0 m below stage values. For tributaries with no gaging stations, stage and river bottom elevations were estimated using the digital elevation model for land surface and constants based on measured stages and river bottom elevations at gaging stations that were available.

The MODFLOW Drain package was used to simulate water discharge from the Upper Floridan aquifer to wetland areas in the local-scale model area. A total of 538 drain cells were specified in layers 5, 6, and 7. Drain cells are located in the northern wetlands (layer 5), northeastern corner (layer 5), and southwestern corner of the model area (model layers 5, 6, and 7), as shown in figure 12. The elevation of drains was initially based approximately on land-surface elevation and stream stage, if available. Drain stages ranged from 3.96 to 6.50 m.

Pumping

The local-scale model area (fig. 13; table 4) has 77 public-supply, industrial, and agricultural wells. Pumping rates during 2000 were used for the steady-state model. Daily total withdrawals from 24 public-supply wells and 53 industrial and agricultural wells were 25,408 m³/d. The average withdrawal rate for the selected PSW was 884 m³/d in 2000. The average

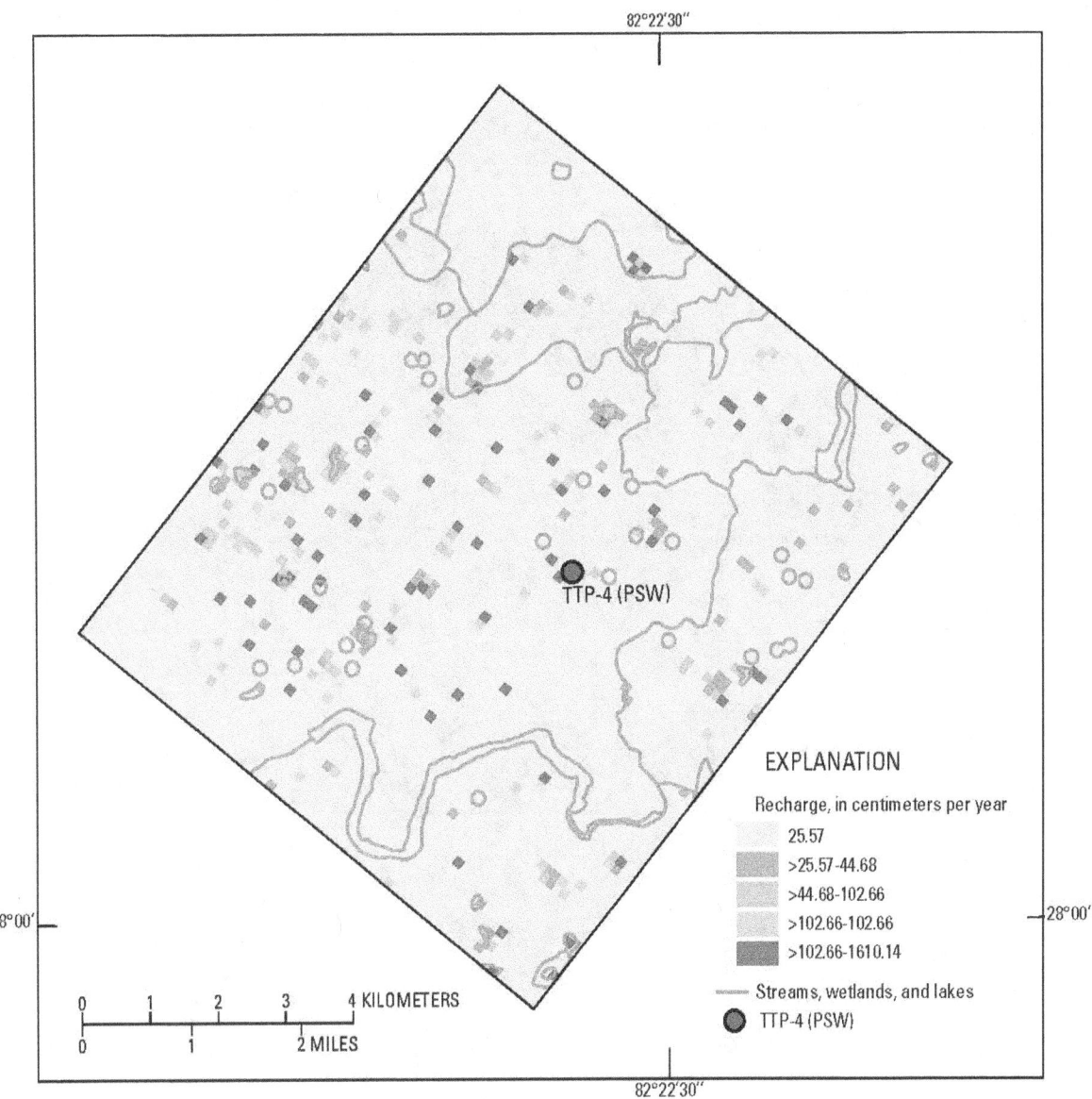

Figure 11. Distribution of recharge in the local-scale study area. PSW is the selected public-supply well.

withdrawal rate for the agricultural and industrial wells of 94 m³/d, was estimated by Sepulveda (2002) and was based on the permitted daily average withdrawal rate. A summary of withdrawal rates by well in the local-scale model area during 2000 is shown in table 4.

Wells are simulated in the local-scale model using the multi-node well package for MODFLOW (Halford and Hanson, 2002). The multi-node well package is used to allow the model to determine the relative contribution of flow from each model layer based on the head and model properties of those layers.

The package also allows for flow to be tracked between specific model layers instead of simply being removed from the simulated aquifer system. Withdrawals are focused in layers 5 to 12. Layer 8, representing the highly transmissive cavernous zone, has 35 percent of the total withdrawals. Layer 12 represents another very productive part of the Upper Floridan aquifer with 33 percent of the total withdrawals. Most of the remaining withdrawals are distributed between layers 5 to 7 and layers 9 to 11. Withdrawals are less than 2 percent for each of the total volumes in layers 3, 4, and 13.

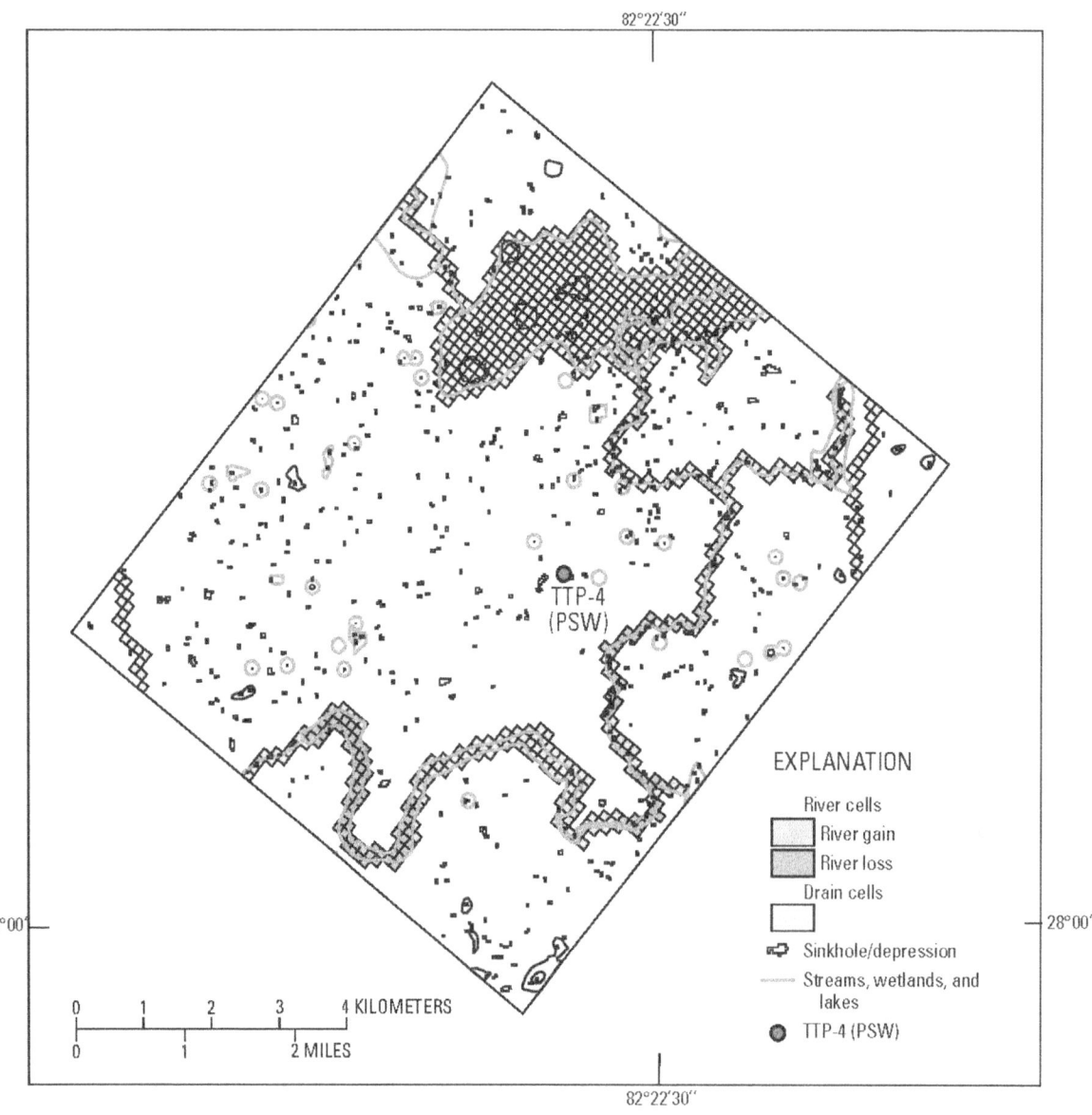

Figure 12. River and drain cells in the local-scale model and study areas. TTP-4 is the selected public-supply well.

Hydraulic and Other Estimated Parameters

Initial estimates for hydraulic parameters and other values in the local-scale model were derived from the calibrated regional model. However, parameters continued to be updated during local-scale model calibration. Initially, trial-and-error methods were used to adjust parameters between model runs, but eventually the model was put into MODFLOW-2000 and finally UCODE to obtain final values for hydraulic parameters, recharge, riverbed and drain conductances, and effective

porosities to maximize the observations (including age tracer information). Eventually, 24 hydraulic, recharge, riverbed and drain conductances, and transport (effective porosities) parameters were used to represent the groundwater flow system in the local-scale model. Finally, 17 parameters were able to be estimated using parameter estimation techniques. Parameter estimates were resolved for recharge and hydraulic conductivities representing the surficial aquifer system and Upper Floridan aquifer and porosities using UCODE (Poeter and others, 2005) and observations of water levels, water-level

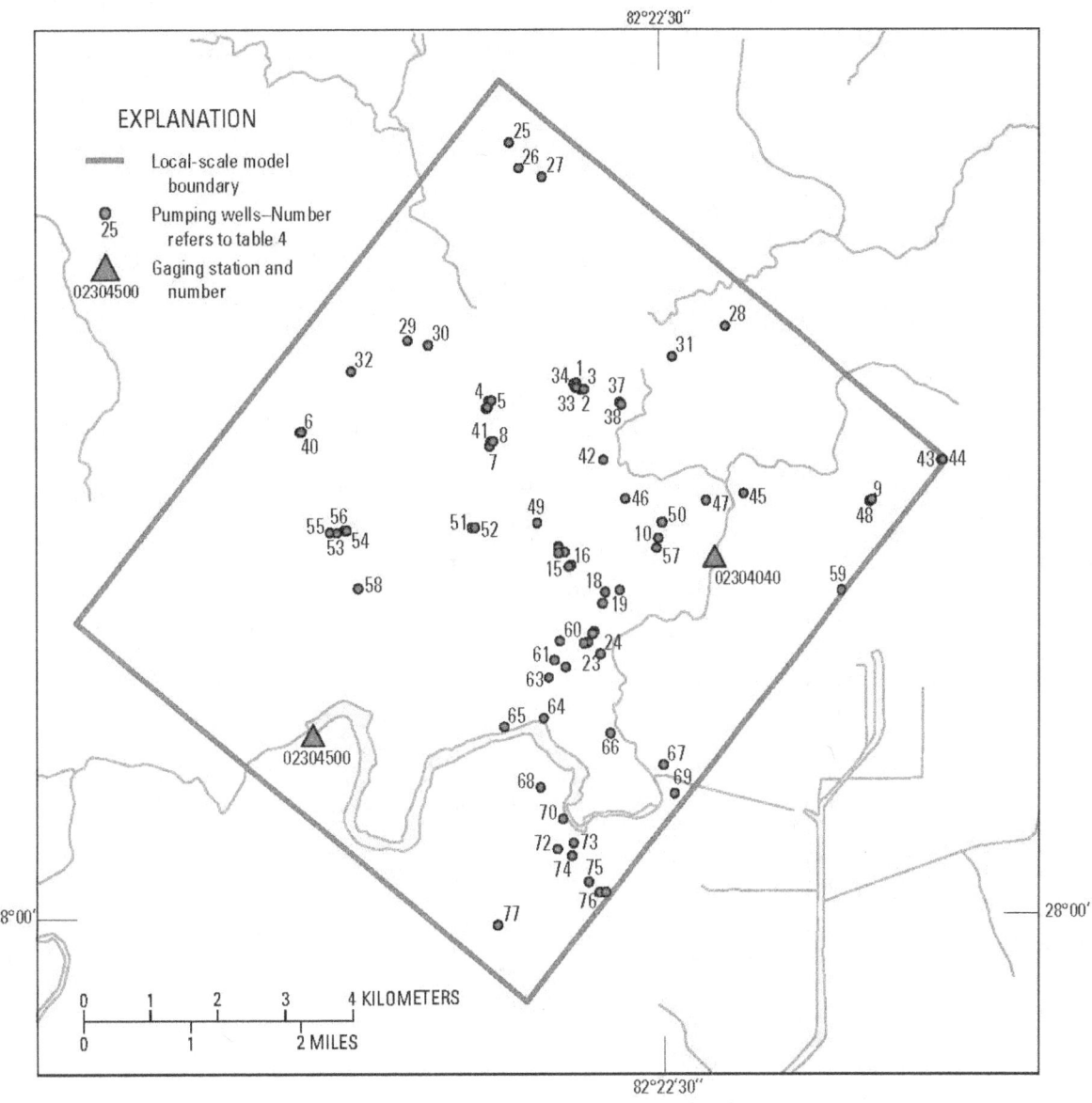

Figure 13. Location of groundwater withdrawal wells and gaging stations in the local-scale study area.

gradients, and age tracer concentrations. Values for riverbed and drain conductances and horizontal hydraulic conductivity for layer 4, representing the intermediate confining unit, were not estimated due to lack of observations.

Generally, hydraulic conductivity parameters in each model layer were conceptualized as a combination of a "base" hydraulic conductivity or recharge value for the porous block with anisotropy applied to vertical and horizontal values in the intermediate confining unit and Upper Floridan aquifer and an adjusted value that applies only to the areas where karst

features have been identified (table 5). For model layers 1 to 3 representing the surficial aquifer system and recharge parameters, multipliers are applied to the hydraulic parameters that are based on the percentage of cell encompassed by one or more closed-basin depressions. For hydraulic parameters in layers 4 to 13 (excluding layer 8) representing the intermediate confining unit and Upper Floridan aquifer, anisotropy and a new greater hydraulic value is usually applied to cells in layers that include a closed-basin depression. Layer 8 has constant and hydraulic properties.

Table 4. Average groundwater withdrawal rates from public-supply wells (wells 1–24), industrial wells, and agricultural wells in the local-scale study area during 2000.

[Locations of wells are shown in fig. 13]

Well number	Elevation of top of open interval (meters)	Elevation of bottom of open interval (meters)	Withdrawal rate (cubic meters per day)	Well number	Elevation of top of open interval (meters)	Elevation of bottom of open interval (meters)	Withdrawal rate (cubic meters per day)
1	6.83	-47.61	261	40	4.79	-25.69	136
2	5.98	-78.95	261	41	5.69	-24.79	57
3	5.07	-31.08	110	42	6.34	-24.14	254
4	-21.38	-31.13	17	43	8.61	-21.87	77
5	-34.33	-80.05	240	44	8.61	-21.87	77
6	-18.81	-140.73	132	45	7.20	-23.28	27
7	-33.50	-146.27	22	46	6.43	-24.05	27
8	6.51	-74.40	32	47	6.95	-23.53	27
9	1.80	-23.92	95	48	8.12	-22.36	98
10	-18.18	-109.62	238	49	5.86	-24.62	27
11	-9.07	-23.39	3,780	50	6.65	-23.83	27
12	-13.74	-25.01	3,901	51	5.43	-25.05	40
13	-28.74	-101.90	1,739	52	5.45	-25.03	40
14	-12.40	-29.47	680	53	4.76	-25.72	353
16	-11.46	-28.22	3,591	54	4.77	-25.71	353
17	-24.35	-126.76	267	55	4.68	-25.80	353
18	-21.34	-126.50	267	56	4.72	-25.76	353
19	-24.27	-125.77	267	57	6.58	-23.90	27
20	-8.61	-126.56	1,701	58	4.68	-25.80	4
21	-5.12	-127.04	1,323	59	7.75	-22.73	27
22	4.22	-100.93	1,134	60	5.87	-24.61	27
23	.12	-77.61	49	61	5.81	-24.67	27
24	5.24	-99.01	340	62	5.87	-24.61	27
25	6.65	-23.83	301	63	5.74	-24.74	23
26	6.56	-23.92	301	64	5.64	-24.84	27
27	6.62	-23.86	261	65	5.37	-25.11	30
28	6.15	-24.33	49	66	6.01	-24.47	27
29	5.52	-24.96	19	67	6.28	-24.20	68
30	5.61	-24.87	19	68	5.49	-24.99	42
31	6.88	-23.60	87	69	6.32	-24.16	23
32	5.17	-25.31	34	70	5.59	-24.89	15
33	6.26	-24.22	121	71	5.66	-24.82	85
34	6.25	-24.23	121	72	5.55	-24.93	8
35	6.29	-24.19	121	73	5.64	-24.84	85
36	5.78	-24.70	125	74	5.62	-24.86	53
37	6.50	-23.98	108	75	5.66	-24.82	33
38	6.51	-23.97	108	76	5.69	-24.79	33
39	5.74	-24.74	125	77	4.81	-25.67	45

Table 5. Hydraulic, recharge, and transport parameters by hydrogeologic unit and model layer used in local-scale groundwater flow and particle-tracking simulations.

[Hydraulic conductivity and recharge, in meters per day; drain and river conductance, in cubic meters per day per meter; cm/yr, centimeters per year; HK, hydraulic conductivity; VK, vertical hydraulic conductivity; HANI, horizontal anistropy; VANI, vertical anistropy]

Model layer	Parameter type	Base value without sinkholes	Base value in depression/karst areas	Description
Surficial Aquifer System				
Layers 1–3	HK	36.78	0.063–36.78	The HK for the surficial aquifer system. The HK in the closed basin depressions varies and is calculated as a percent of cell in the depression basin. The values are considerably lower than non-depression areas, which probably is due to the altered structure of the surficial aquifer system compared to undisturbed areas
	VK	0.3678	0.063	The VK for the surficial aquifer system is calculated as HK divided by the VANI. In areas of depressions, VANI is 1.0. Outside of depressions the VANI is 100.0
	Effective porosity	0.322	0.322	Porosity for the surficial aquifer system
Intermediate Confining Unit				
Layer 4	HK	0.0103	0.0103	The HK for the intermediate confining unit
	VK	4.5×10^{-5}	541	The VK for the intermediate confining unit. In areas with depressions and along the river and drains, the higher value is used; otherwise the lower value is used
	Effective porosity	0.011	0.004	The estimated number is lower than expected probably due to preferential flow paths
Upper Floridan Aquifer				
Layers 5–7	HK	36.96 (rows), 15.63 (columns)	36.96 (rows), 15.63 (columns)	The HK for the upper part of the Upper Floridan aquifer. Because anisotropy is used, there is one conductivity along rows (northwest to southeast) and another along columns. The hydraulic conductivity along columns is calculated as (HANI = 0.423)*HK along rows
	VK	0.0424	541	The VK for the Upper Floridan aquifer. The VK uses the high value in areas of depressions, drains, and the river and uses the base value everywhere else
	Effective porosity	0.12	0.004	Effective porosity of the Upper Floridan aquifer. If a depression is present, the lower value is used; otherwise 0.12 is used
Layer 8	HK	674 (rows), 74.95 (columns)	674 (rows), 74.95 (columns)	The HK for the Upper Floridan aquifer in layer 8. Because anisotropy is used, this is the conductivity along rows (northwest to southeast). The HK along columns is calculated as the HANI * HK(rows) = HK(columns); (HANI = 0.1105)
	VK	541	541	The VK for layer 8
	Effective porosity	0.004	0.004	Porosity for layer 8. The low value would indicate that the actual volume in which the conduit flow takes place is small
Layers 9–13	HK	36.96 (row), 15.63 (column)	36.96 (row), 15.63 (column)	The HK for the lower part of the modeled Upper Floridan aquifer. Because anisotropy is used, there is one conductivity along rows and another along columns (HANI = 0.423)
	VK	0.0424	456	The VK for the lower part of the modeled Upper Floridan aquifer. The VK uses a higher value (541 meter per day) where there are drain cells on the western edge of the modeled area. The model uses the lower value elsewhere
	Effective porosity	0.12	0.12	Porosity of the porous block in the lower modeled Upper Floridan aquifer

Table 5. (Continued) Hydraulic, recharge, and transport parameters by hydrogeologic unit and model layer used in local-scale groundwater flow and particle-tracking simulations.

[Hydraulic conductivity and recharge, in meters per day; drain and river conductance, in cubic meters per day per meter, cm/yr, centimeters per year; HK, hydraulic conductivity; VK, vertical hydraulic conductivity; HANI, horizontal anistropy; VANI, vertical anistropy]

Model layer	Parameter type	Base value without sinkholes	Base value in depression/karst areas	Description
			Other Hydraulic and Stress Properties	
Layers 1–5	Recharge	0.0007 (or 25.6 cm/yr)	0.00052 (or 19 cm/yr karst multiplier)	The base recharge (25.6 cm/yr) is applied everywhere; however, in areas of depressions, this base value is increased by a value (19 cm/yr) multiplied by a percentage based on the area of the depression that contributes recharge to the cell. This number is added to the base recharge
			Drain and Riverbed Conductance Parameters and Values	
Layers 5–7	Drain conductance	0.0010–0.000010	0.001–100,000	Parameters factor multipliers—0.001 used for the northern wetlands—conductances from regional model multiplied by the parameter value. Parameter values are 1,000 for the northeastern drains, and 100,000 for the southwestern drains to force boundary flow into agreement with the regional flow model
Layers 3, 5	Riverbed conductance	39.6	39.6–2,185.7	River cells in layers 3 above the dam and in layer 5 below the dam. Riverbed conductances from regional model multiplied by this constant factor multiplier

Hydraulic Parameters

The horizontal hydraulic conductivity for model layers 1 to 3, representing the surficial aquifer system, ranges from 0.06 to 36.78 m/d (fig. 14; table 5). The values for individual cells are derived by adding together two horizontal hydraulic conductivity terms: one for cells with sinkholes and one for cells without sinkholes. Each conductivity value is prorated by the percentage of the cell with undisturbed or disturbed (sinkholes) porous media. The base horizontal hydraulic conductivity value for undisturbed porous media is 36.78 m/d, whereas the base horizontal hydraulic conductivity value for cells that are entirely encompassed by sinkholes is 0.063 m/d. For example, a model cell entirely encompassed by a depression has a horizontal hydraulic conductivity of 0.06 m/d; a cell entirely without sinkholes has a hydraulic conductivity value of 36.78 m/d. A cell that is 50-percent sinkhole and 50-percent undisturbed porous media would have a horizontal hydraulic conductivity of 18.42 m/d. Horizontal anisotropy was not specified for layers 1 to 3, representing the surficial aquifer system, because presumably there is no preferential direction of flow in this relatively homogenous sand-and-gravel aquifer.

The vertical hydraulic conductivity for layers 1 to 3 varies inversely with the horizontal hydraulic conductivity (vertical hydraulic conductivity equals horizontal hydraulic conductivity divided by the vertical anisotropy value). The horizontal hydraulic conductivity is divided by 100, so that it equals 0.37 m/d in cells without sinkholes. The vertical

hydraulic conductivity is 0.063/1.0 m/d or 0.063 m/d in cells with sinkholes. Vertical hydraulic conductivity values range from 0.063 to 0.37 m/d, increasing in undisturbed sediments. This may reflect disturbed beds and disruption to transport through these layers.

The horizontal hydraulic conductivity for layer 4, representing the intermediate confining unit, is either 0.0103 or 1.03 m/d. The base value for undisturbed porous media is 0.0103 m/d, but where sinkholes are present (fig. 14), the hydraulic conductivity is multiplied by 100. The base vertical hydraulic conductivity for the intermediate confining unit is 4.5×10^{-5} m/d derived in the local-scale model calibration. However, in depression areas and under the river and drains, this value, derived in UCODE, is specified at 541 m/d to simulate the rapid transmission of water through short-circuiting mechanisms (sinkholes). Anisotropy was not estimated for this layer due to the sparse number of observations and insensitivity of the parameters associated with layer 4.

The base horizontal hydraulic conductivity for layers 5 through 13 (except for layer 8), representing the Upper Floridan aquifer, is 15.63 m/d along columns and 36.96 m/d along rows (table 5). The horizontal hydraulic conductivity anisotropy was estimated in UCODE as 0.423. This strong tendency toward anisotropy controls flow path lines and shifts much of the simulated flow along rows (northwest to southeast) in the model grid, which is consistent with previous studies and photolineament work (Langevin, 1998). Vertical hydraulic

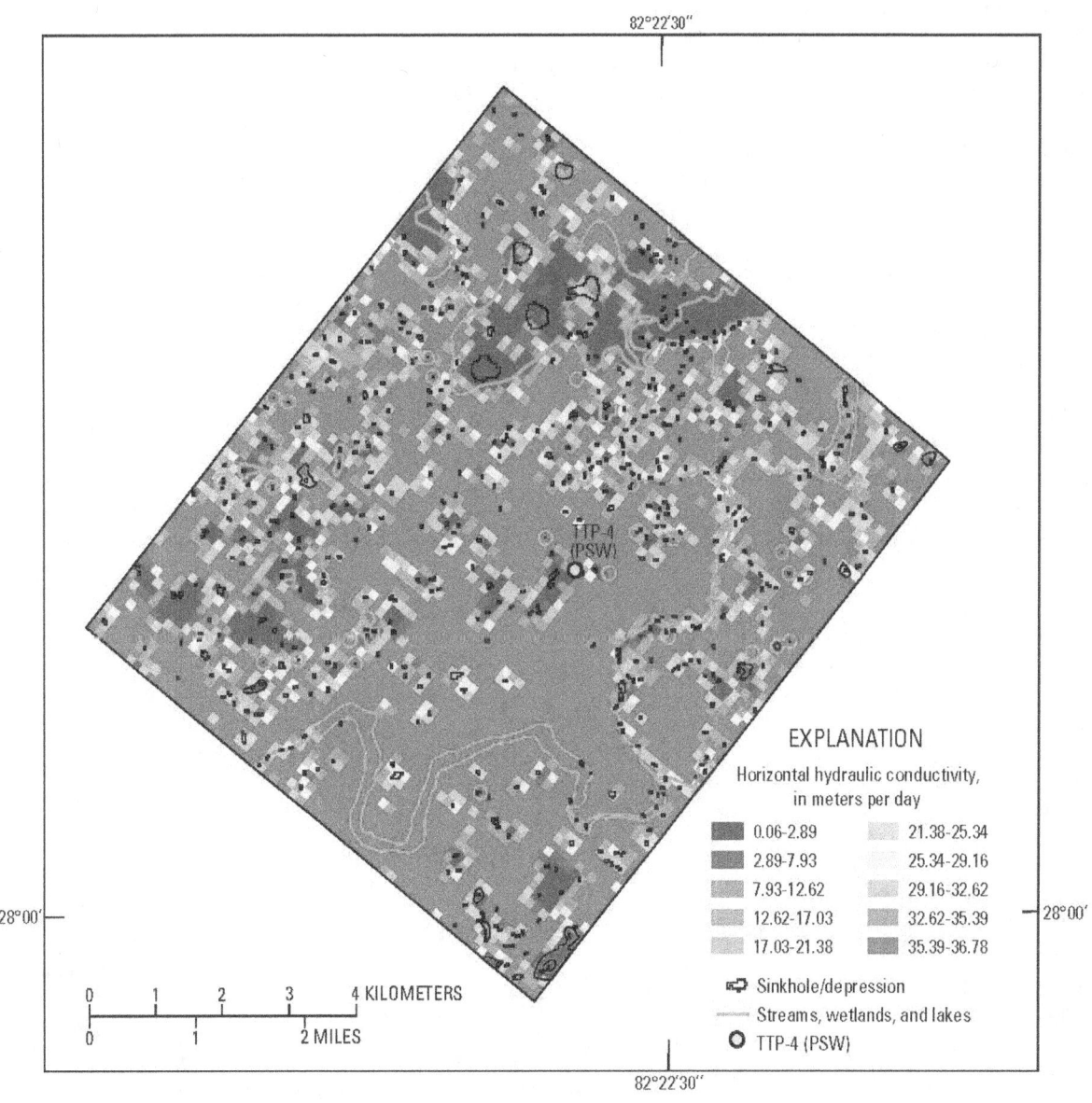

82°22'30"

TTP-4
(PSW)

EXPLANATION

Horizontal hydraulic conductivity,
in meters per day

0.06-2.89	21.38-25.34
2.89-7.93	25.34-29.16
7.93-12.62	29.16-32.62
12.62-17.03	32.62-35.39
17.03-21.38	35.39-36.78

Sinkhole/depression

Streams, wetlands, and lakes

O TTP-4 (PSW)

28°00'   28°00'

0   1   2   3   4 KILOMETERS

0   1   2 MILES

82°22'30"

Figure 14. Distribution of horizontal hydraulic conductivity in model layers 1 to 3, representing the surficial aquifer system. PSW is the selected public-supply well.

conductivity is specified at 0.0424 m/d in the porous block and 541 m/d in sinkholes, along the river, and under drains in layers 5 to 7. In layers 9 to 13, the vertical hydraulic conductivity is specified at 0.0424 m/d everywhere, except under the western drain where the vertical hydraulic conductivity is 541 m/d. In layers 5 to 7 representing the top of the Tampa Member, there is no adjustment for sinkholes—only the row/column anisotropy.

Layer 8 represents the highly transmissive cavernous layer in the approximate middle of the Tampa Member (the top unit of the Upper Floridan aquifer). The horizontal hydraulic conductivity of this layer is 674 m/d along the rows and 74.95 m/d along the columns (table 5). The value for the horizontal hydraulic conductivity anisotropy resolved in UCODE is 0.1105 (table 5). The vertical hydraulic conductivity also resolved in UCODE is 541 m/d throughout the layer.

Four additional hydraulic parameters, one for riverbed conductance and three for drain conductance (table 5), were simulated but not estimated with UCODE due to a lack of observations. Initial riverbed conductances were taken from the regional-scale model, but were then multiplied by a riverbed conductance parameter to increase the values for the local-scale model. The riverbed conductance parameter multiplier is specified at 39.6 for all model river reaches. Final riverbed conductances ranged from 39.6 to 2,185.7 m^3/d per meter with a median value of 524.6 m^3/d per meter. Drain conductances varied for each drain area. One drain parameter multiplier was specified for the central-north wetlands area (0.001). The net result of this parameter multiplier is that the drain conductance varies from 0.001 to 15.63 m^3/d per meter in this drain area. The other two drain parameters are specified constants of 1,000 for the northeastern drains area and 100,000 for the southwestern drains area in the local-scale model. These drain conductances originated from the regional-scale model and need to be set high to match observed hydraulic heads in the local-scale and regional-scale models.

Recharge Parameters

Recharge is simulated as the sum of two parameters values, and both were estimated using UCODE. The first recharge parameter represents an areal recharge value (0.0007 m/d—25.6 cm/yr) applied to all cells, representing a base areal recharge value that would be expected to occur through infiltration of precipitation throughout the local-scale model area (table 5). The second recharge parameter represents an additional or focused recharge value that would be expected to occur in cells that contain closed-basin depressions. The second recharge parameter is a combination of a constant (0.00052 m/d—18.99 cm/yr) multiplied by the percentage of the ACR located in the closed-basin depression. Recharge is increased in cells that contain closed-basin depressions to try to mimic the focusing effects of sinkholes on recharge, because cells with sinkholes may drain a much larger area than one cell. Drainage basins for sinkholes can be very large. For example, if a sinkhole drains a 16-cell area, the recharge rate would be about 100 cm/yr for the entire sinkhole drainage basin. Final recharge totals for each cell is given by the sum of these two recharge parameters. Total recharge values for each model-grid cell ranged from 25.67 to 1,610.14 cm/yr per cell (fig. 11). Most of the model-grid cells (95 percent) had a total recharge value of 25.57 cm/yr (base areal value). Only 55 model-grid cells (less than 1 percent) had total recharge values greater than 278.08 cm/yr.

Other Parameters

Model parameters controlling velocities and, therefore, particle-tracking age and tracer concentration results from the local-scale model include effective porosities for the groundwater flow system. Initial effective porosity values were based on literature values obtained in Knochenmus and Robinson (1996) and Langevin (1998), but were updated using the measured age tracer concentrations (sulfur hexafluoride and tritium) at the monitoring wells and the selected PSW as observations in the nonlinear regression using UCODE.

Final effective porosities were specified for each active cell according to the layer/aquifer/karst feature defined for that cell. Generally, the final effective estimated porosities used in this modeling effort are at the low end of a range of porosity values given in the literature (Domenico and Schwartz, 1990). A base effective porosity of 0.322 is used throughout layers 1 to 3, representing the surficial aquifer system (table 5). The base effective porosity for layer 4, representing the intermediate confining unit, is 0.011; however, a value of 0.004 is used in the depressions. The calibrated base effective porosity for layer 4 is lower than expected based on values of about 0.30 for clays in Domenica and Schwartz (1990), and may suggest that preferential flow paths are the main mechanism of flow through the clay layer. The base effective porosity for layer 5 through 13 (except for layer 8), representing the Upper Floridan aquifer, is 0.12; however, a value of 0.004 is used in layers 5 to 7 where there are depressions and throughout layer 8. Similar to the porosity in layer 4, the low value of 0.004 suggests that the flow occurs only in a small percentage of the total volume of the aquifer, which is consistent with the concept of flow through conduits. All flow paths for the selected PSW and monitoring wells are within the areal extent of the local-scale model.

Parameter Sensitivity

The number and location of observations used in the model calibration affect parameter sensitivities and are directly responsible for which parameters can be estimated using parameter estimation (UCODE; Poeter and others, 2005). The two recharge parameters at 97.4 and 38.7 percent are the most sensitive parameters in the simulation (fig. 15). Other sensitive parameters are horizontal hydraulic conductivity and anisotropy of the Upper Floridan aquifer at 16.5 and 12.7, respectively. Other somewhat sensitive parameters include horizontal hydraulic conductivity and anisotropy for layers 5 to 13 (excluding layer 8), riverbed conductance, effective porosity, and the vertical hydraulic conductivity for layer 4. Other parameters with sensitivities less than 10 percent include the hydraulic conductivity and anisotropy for layer 8 (highly transmissive cavernous zone in the Upper Floridan aquifer), anisotropy for layer 4 (intermediate confining unit), effective porosity and drain parameters, and hydraulic conductivity pertaining to layers 1 to 3 (surficial aquifer system).

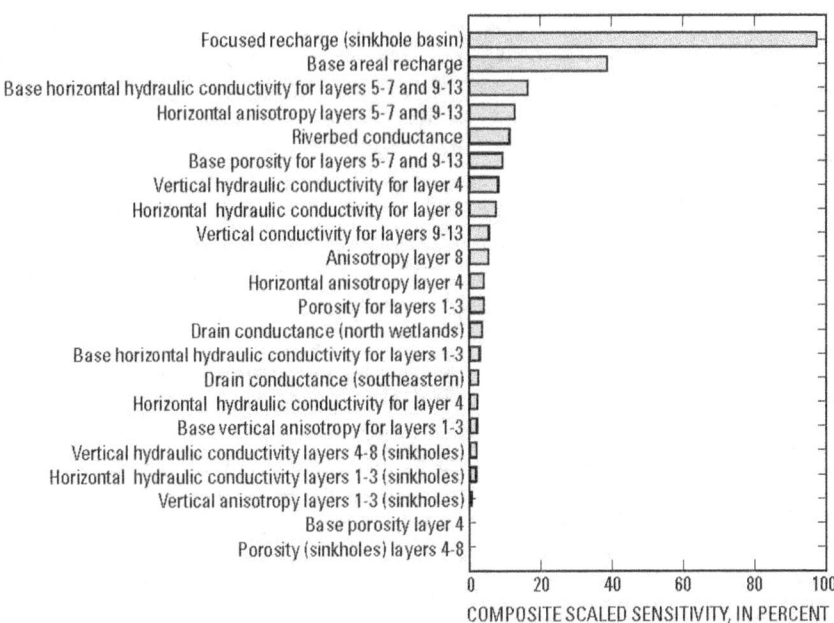

Figure 15. Composite scaled sensitivity of the parameters used to calibrate the groundwater flow and transport model in UCODE.

Simulation of Particle Tracking

Particle tracking was used to compute flow paths and advective traveltimes throughout the model area and to delineate the ACR and zone of contribution for the selected PSW. The ACR to a discharging well is defined as the area at the top of the water table where recharging water that enters the groundwater flow system will eventually be removed by the well. The zone of contribution is defined as the specific volume of aquifer material bounded by outermost flow paths that will recharge a discharging well (Focazio and others, 2002). These results were used to characterize the sources of recharge water reaching the well. Steady-state transport was assumed and recharge rates for individual particles of water entering the well were estimated from the simulated traveltimes. The recharge rates were combined with estimated input concentrations of several tracers (tritium, sulfur hexafluoride, and nitrate) to calculate flux-weighted concentrations of the tracers reaching the well. The resulting calculated concentrations were compared with measured concentrations to evaluate the adequacy of the model to simulate advective transport and, thereby, address several project objectives. Such objectives include: (1) assessing the effects of natural factors and human activities on contaminant occurrence in PSWs, and (2) providing information to managers so they can develop more effective strategies to deal with contamination problems affecting selected PSWs.

Particle tracking was performed using MODPATH, which uses cellular volumetric fluxes from a groundwater flow model and effective porosity to calculate linear velocity. The x, y, and z components of linear velocity are used to generate a velocity field using simple linear interpolation of the components between adjacent cell faces of the finite-difference cells. For steady-state simulations, an analytical expression for the flow path in each cell is calculated by direct integration of the velocity components. The traveltime calculated by this method represents an average traveltime for the advection of a "particle" of water or a conservative solute. Dispersion, diffusion, adsorption, retardation, degradation or any other transport process affecting the concentrations of contaminant constituents are not included in the MODPATH simulation for determining traveltimes of water. The simulated ages of water particles at a well are computed by tracing water particles either backward from the monitoring well toward the ACR or forward from the ACR to the open-interval of the selected PSW.

To calculate concentrations of tracers for parameter estimation, particle tracking was used to obtain a distribution of particle ages that were then associated with known input functions. A backward-tracking approach was used to obtain the age distributions. For the monitoring wells, 10 particles were evenly distributed in a vertical line over the open interval of a monitoring well. Particles were tracked backward toward the area of recharge. For the selected PSW, 100 particles, distributed on each cell face, were tracked using the backward particle tracking mode.

Each particle is associated with an end point and final traveltime, a flow pathline, and traveltime along the flow pathline. In addition,, the ACR and the zone of contribution are mapped from the resultant collection of flow pathlines and intersected with land-use coverages to identify current and potential sources of contaminants to the wells. Statistical information about land use in each ACR and the zone of contribution was computed and is described by Crandall (2007).

Calibration

Groundwater flow model and particle tracking calibration was achieved using 53 groundwater levels and gradient observations and 19 sulfur hexafluoride concentrations. Overall, 24 parameters were used to define the simulation, including those for horizontal and vertical hydraulic conductivity, anisotropy, recharge, riverbed and drain conductance, effective porosity using UCODE (Poeter and others, 2005), a universal code for sensitivity, calibration (using parameter estimation), and uncertainty evaluations in concert with MODFLOW and MODPATH (Pollack, 1994). Only 17 of 24 parameters could be estimated in parameter estimation, which ultimately was due to insensitivity of the parameters (lack of critical observations). Estimated parameter values minimize the sum of squares differences between observed and simulated values to result in the best match between measured and simulated water levels, water-level gradients, and age tracer concentrations. No river leakage was used to calibrate the model, because all of the streamflow data for the Hilllsborough River was from the period before the construction of the Hillsborough River Reservoir Dam. In addition, there were no drain leakage observations to help calibrate the drain parameters.

The average weighted residual for all observations is -0.261. Some minor bias in the model exists as 38 residuals are greater than or equal to observed values and 53 residuals are less than observed values. Model residuals are smallest for water level and water-level gradients. There was a -0.01 percent discrepancy in the overall water budget (1.79199 m³/s). Age-tracer concentrations matched well enough to suggest a reasonably good representation of the porosity and hydraulic parameters. Water levels, water-level gradients, flow patterns, and water budget components were used in the calibration of the groundwater flow model. These parameters are discussed in detail in the subsequent sections.

Water Levels and Water-Level Gradients

The groundwater flow model was calibrated using 42 water-level observations. Water-level data came from various sources including TANC, City of Temple Terrace, and the Southwest Florida Water Management District (table 6). There were 28 water-level measurements from wells open to the Upper Floridan aquifer, 2 water-level measurements from wells open to the intermediate confining unit, and 12 water-level measurements from wells open to the surficial aquifer system. Water-level gradients also were used to help calibrate the model; 7 were between the upper and lower parts of the Upper Floridan aquifer, and 5 were between the surficial aquifer system and Upper Floridan aquifer. Water-level gradient observations were computed from wells in well nest: GARC, LRP, MAS, 62SRP, RP, THC, and WP. Weights used for water levels and gradients ranged from 0.20 to 2.00 (table 6).

Nonweighted simulated hydraulic heads and hydraulic head gradients open to layers 1 to 3 (representing the surficial aquifer system) and one well open to layer 4 (representing the intermediate confining unit) matched the observed groundwater level and gradient measurements slightly worse than wells open to layers 5 to 13, representing the Upper Floridan aquifer (table 6; figs. 16, 17). The surficial aquifer system residuals ranged from -1.91 to 3.57 m (table 6) and had a median residual of -0.28 m; the Upper Floridan aquifer residuals ranged from -1.80 to 1.71 m and had a median residual of 0.04 m. Observed water levels matched the simulated water levels best for Upper Floridan aquifer well 113RC-F190 (residual of less than 0.01 m) and in surficial aquifer system wells at LP-S30 and 113RC-S35. The simulated water levels were 7.25 m in 113RC-H50m, the only well in the intermediate confining unit with a continuous recorder; observed water level was 7.37 m. The residuals of water-level gradients from the surficial aquifer system to the Upper Floridan aquifer ranged from -0.87 to -0.17 m; all of the simulated and weighted water-level gradients were slightly larger than the nonweighted residuals or observed values. Median water-level residuals in the local-scale TANC observation wells open to the surficial aquifer system or the intermediate confining unit were approximately balanced between simulated values that were lower and higher than observed values.

Simulated hydraulic head and hydraulic head gradient values from wells open to the Upper Floridan aquifer matched the observed water levels reasonably well (table 6; fig. 18). Simulated water levels in wells open to the Upper Floridan aquifer ranged from 4.85 to 8.6 m, whereas observed water levels ranged from 4.43 to 9.8 m. In the middle of the model area where most of the observation wells are located, the model fit improved (fig. 18). For example, well 113RC-F190 had a residual water level of less than 0.01 m. Well WP-F299, the deepest monitoring well in the Upper Floridan aquifer installed for the TANC study, had a simulated water level of 6.3 m and an observed water level of 6.19 m. The simulated median water levels in 13 wells open to the Upper Floridan aquifer were greater than the observed median water levels and less than the observed water levels in 14 wells. Water-level residuals ranged from -1.8 to 1.71 m and the median weighted residual was 0.05 m.

Flow Patterns

The simulated potentiometric surface of the water table, which in most areas is composed of part of the surficial aquifer system but in lower lying areas is composed of the Upper Floridan aquifer, was generally representative of the measured water-table surface in the local-scale model area. Water flowed from the northern corner of the model area toward the south and southeast. The simulated water-table surface was highest in layers 1 to 3 (8.5 m) in the northeastern corner of the model area boundary and the northwestern side of the model area on the terrace (fig. 19A). Most of layer 1

Table 6. Measured and simulated hydraulic heads and hydraulic head gradients, in the local-scale model, and residual, weighted residual, aquifer, and data source for monitoring wells.

[Hydraulic heads, in meters. TANC, Transport of Anthropogenic and Natural Contaminants; SWFWMD, Southwest Florida Water Management District; CTT, City of Temple Terrace. PSW is the selected public-supply well]

Observation name	Observed value	Simulated value	Residual	Weighted residual	Data source
Hydraulic head—Upper Floridan aquifer					
GARC-F200	6.63	6.74	-0.12	-0.16	TANC
GARC-F75	6.23	6.85	-.62	-.88	TANC
LRP-F160	7.4	5.79	1.61	2.28	TANC
LRP-H105	7.41	6.29	1.12	1.58	TANC
MAS-R-F160	7.44	5.73	1.71	2.42	TANC
MAS-R-F64	6.78	5.66	1.12	1.58	TANC
113RC-F190	6.85	6.84	.00763	.0108	TANC
113RC-H50	7.02	6.15	.88	1.24	TANC
62SRP-H55	8.1	7.29	.81	1.14	TANC
RP-F103	6.56	6.7	-.15	-.22	TANC
RP-F77	6.56	6.71	-.14	-.2	TANC
TTP-4 (PSW)	6.73	5.47	1.26	1.79	TANC
THC-F197	6.81	6.55	.25	.36	TANC
THC-F75	6.82	6.63	.19	.26	TANC
WP-F299	6.19	6.3	-.11	-.15	TANC
WP-F150	6.24	5.73	.5	.71	TANC
CHOOL_WELL_1	9.8	8.29	1.51	2.13	SWFWMD
DGE_17_DEEP	9.43	8.6	.83	1.18	SWFWMD
K_FLORIDAN	6.87	7.57	-.7	-1	SWFWMD
MPA	4.43	4.85	-.42	-.6	SWFWMD
UNNAMED_1	5.19	5.89	-.7	-.99	SWFWMD
UNNAMED_2	5.37	5.71	-.34	-.48	SWFWMD
WELL#12	6.25	6.12	.13	.18	CTT
WELL#9	5.88	6.15	-.27	-.38	CTT
WOODMONT	6.32	6.25	.0658	.0931	CTT
ON_PARK	5.91	7.71	-1.8	-2.54	SWFWMD
SERENA	5.85	7.18	-1.33	-1.88	CTT
GRADE_ORANGE_SU	5.61	6.53	-.91	-1.28	SWFWMD
Hydraulic head—Surficial aquifer system					
BBP-S45	7.47	8.47	-.99	-1.41	TANC
GARC-S23	6.63	7.42	-.79	-1.12	TANC
JARP-S40	6.01	6.96	-.95	-1.34	TANC
Hydraulic head gradient—Upper Floridan aquifer (upper to lower part)					
GARC-UL	-.4	.11	-.51	-.72	TANC
LRP-UL	.0100	.51	-.5	-.7	TANC
MAS-UL	-.66	-.640	-.6	-.84	TANC
62SRP-UL	1.071	1.14	-.700	-.989	TANC
RP-UL	.0110	.00155	.00945	.0134	TANC
THC-UL	.013	.0810	-.680	-.961	TANC
WP-UL	.0420	-.56	.61	.86	TANC

Table 6. (Continued) Measured and simulated hydraulic heads and hydraulic head gradients, in the local-scale model, and residual, weighted residual, aquifer, and data source for monitoring wells.

[Hydraulic heads, in meters. TANC, Transport of Anthropogenic and Natural Contaminants; SWFWMD, Southwest Florida Water Management District; CTT, City of Temple Terrace. PSW is the selected public-supply well]

Observation name	Observed value	Simulated value	Residual	Weighted residual	Data source
Hydraulic head gradient—Surficial aquifer system to the Upper Floridan aquifer					
GARC-SF	.4	.56	-.17	-.23	TANC
113RC-SF	.46	.75	-.28	-.4	TANC
RP-SF	.1	.48	-.38	-.53	TANC
TCH-SF	.016	.88	-.87	-1.23	TANC
WP-SF	2.15	2.84	-.7	-.98	TANC
LRP-S25	18.1	20	-1.91	-.85	TANC
LP-S30	8.56	8.52	.0330	.0467	TANC
MAS-R-S30	12.65	9.08	3.57	1.59	TANC
113RC-S35	7.31	7.59	-.28	-.39	TANC
QRP-S20	8.64	7.22	1.41	2	TANC
RP-S20	6.67	7.19	-.52	-.73	TANC
THC-SA/H46[1]	6.83	7.52	-.68	-.97	TANC
WP-S64	8.38	8.58	-.2	-.28	TANC
62SRP-S34	13.37	12.71	.66	.29	TANC
113RC-H50[2]	7.33	7.25	.0767	.11	TANC

[1]THC-SA penetrates the surficial aquifer system, and H46 penetrates the intermediate confining unit.
[2]113RC-H50 penetrates the intermediate confining unit.

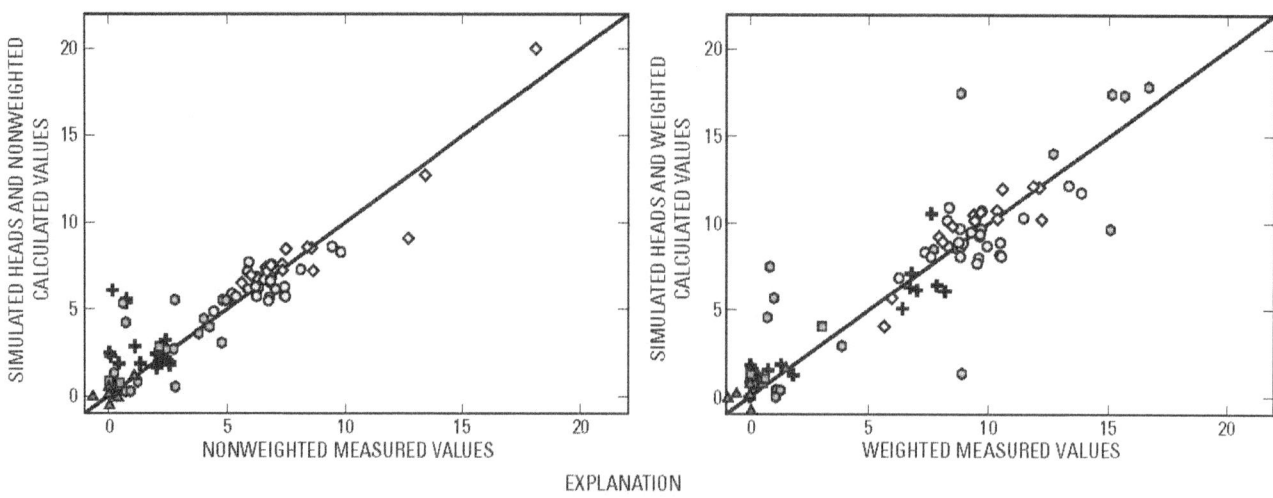

EXPLANATION

○ Upper Floridan aquifer heads, in meters
▲ Upper Floridan aquifer to surficial aquifer system gradients, in meters
▥ Surficial aquifer system to Upper Floridan Aquifer gradients, in meters

◇ Surficial aquifer system heads, in meters
⬡ Sulfur hexafluoride age tracer concentration, in volumetric parts per trillion
✚ Tritium age tracer concentration, in tritium units

Figure 16. Simulated and measured hydraulic heads, hydraulic head gradients, sulfur hexafluoride and tritium concentrations, and corresponding weighted/nonweighted simulated and measured values.

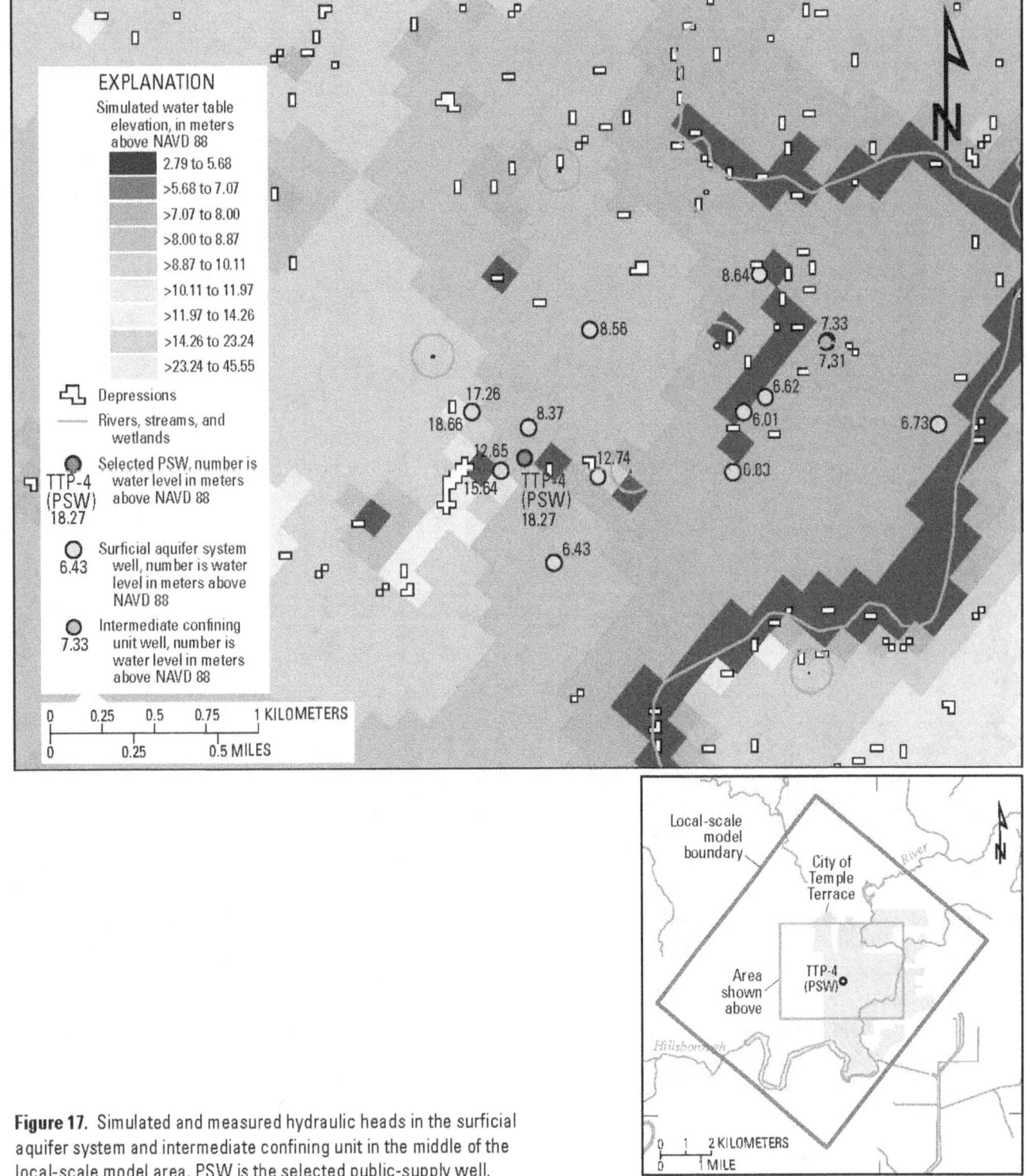

Figure 17. Simulated and measured hydraulic heads in the surficial aquifer system and intermediate confining unit in the middle of the local-scale model area. PSW is the selected public-supply well.

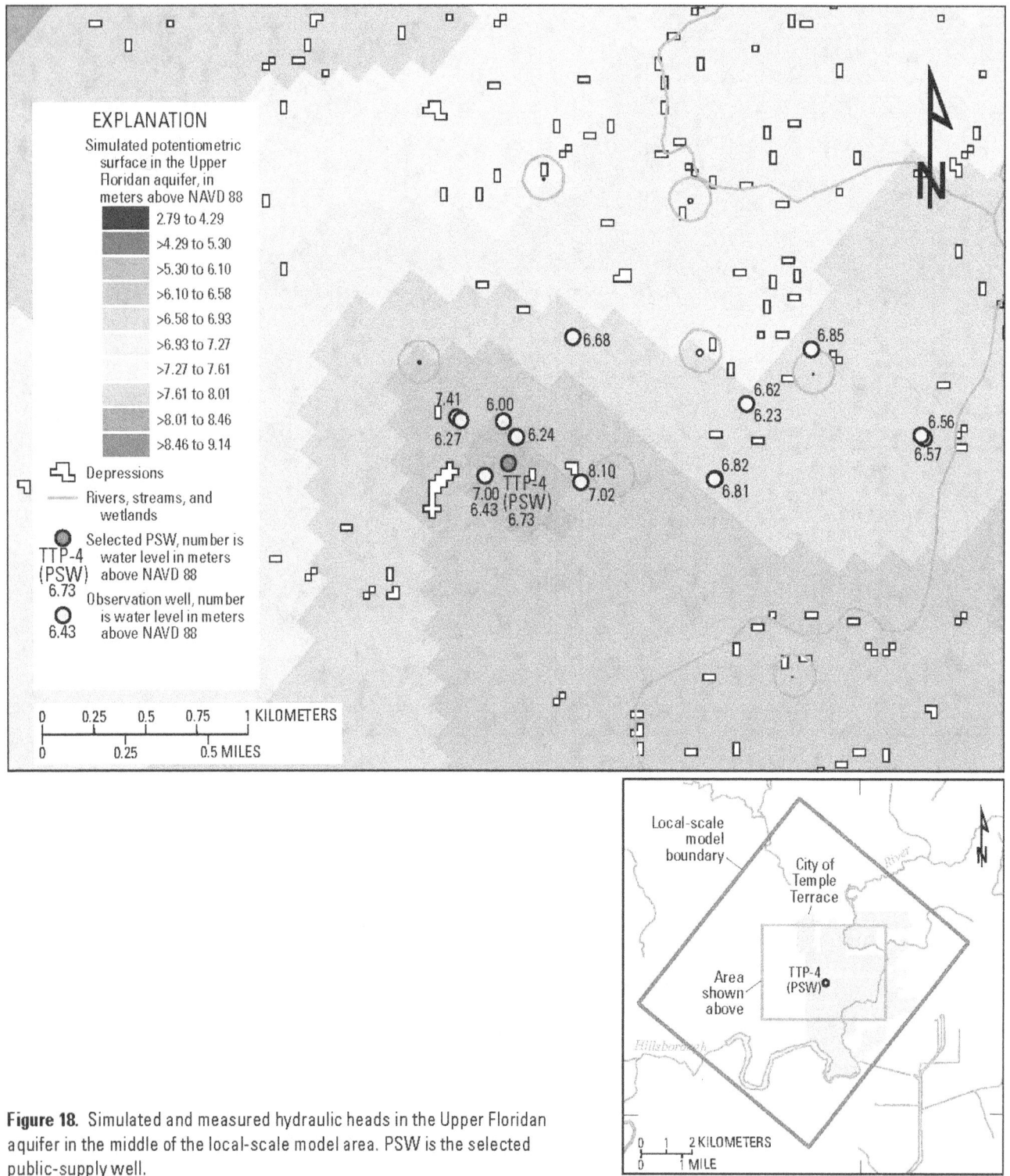

Figure 18. Simulated and measured hydraulic heads in the Upper Floridan aquifer in the middle of the local-scale model area. PSW is the selected public-supply well.

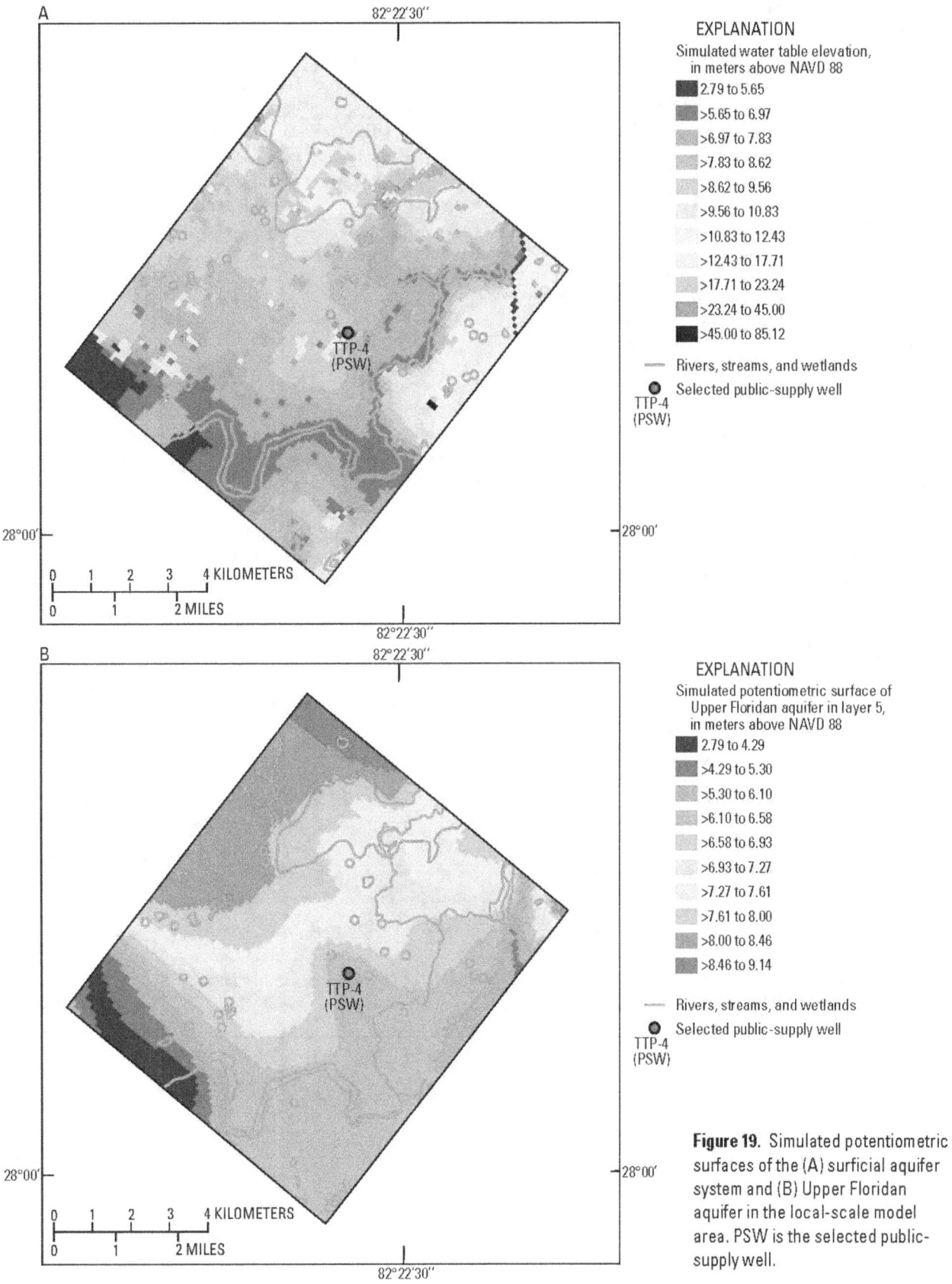

Figure 19. Simulated potentiometric surfaces of the (A) surficial aquifer system and (B) Upper Floridan aquifer in the local-scale model area. PSW is the selected public-supply well.

and some of layer 2 were unsaturated, so the corresponding cells were made inactive on the terrace. Simulated hydraulic heads in layers 1 to 3 ranged from 2.79 to 85.12 m (fig. 19A). The highest simulated hydraulic head occurred in only one cell in the southeastern and southwestern parts of the model area. The second and third highest simulated hydraulic head values (45.2 and 40.9 m) occurred in one cell each—next to the highest hydraulic head cell and near the selected PSW. These cells are areas of focused recharge that likely are bigger in size than the model cell or do not drain an area as large as the digital elevation model would indicate. The fourth highest simulated hydraulic head was 22.8 m.

The simulated potentiometric surface of the Upper Floridan aquifer followed the measured potentiometric surface of the Upper Floridan aquifer based on median calendar year 2000 water levels (figs. 18 and 19B). Generally, water flowed from the northern and northeastern parts of the local-scale model area toward the southern and southeastern parts. The highest simulated hydraulic heads occurred on the northwestern part of the model area; on the boundary, outflow occurred through the southeastern and southwestern parts of the local-scale model area. The ranges in hydraulic heads fit observed hydraulic heads reasonably well. The hydraulic head decreased from north to south and southeast across the local-scale model area, in good agreement with the general observed flow direction.

Water Budget

The simulated water budget has two main components of inflow (recharge and specified boundary flows) and four net outflow components (specified boundary flows, drains, river leakage, and multi-node wells) to the model area (table 7). The simulated water budget is also in agreement with regional studies for recharge, specified boundary flows, and river leakage where data are available. Total inflow is 154,828.34 m³/d, including inflow from recharge, specified boundary flows, river leakage, and multi-node wells.

Recharge contributes 79,756.98 m³/d into the model and accounts for more than 51.5 percent of total inflows (table 7). There is a net specified influx across the model boundaries of 59,574.94 m³/d, which is about 5.6 percent of the total inflow. Outflow discharges include flow out of lateral model boundaries, drains, river leakage, and withdrawals by wells. The total discharge to drains is 45,189.46 m³/d, or 29.2 percent of the total outflow. River leakage is variable by cell within the model, but overall there is more outflow than inflow. The net river leakage is 21,442.81 m³/d. Most of the leakage from the aquifer to the river occurs near the bottom of the reservoir.

Particle Tracking

A summary of final steady-state traveltimes for each particle reaching the monitoring wells or the selected PSW was obtained from MODPATH and used to describe the distribution of simulated particle ages associated with recharge water reaching the wells. A tracer concentration was assigned to each particle on the basis of the recharge date (from particle ages) and the concentration of each age tracer in the atmosphere at the time of recharge (minus radioactive decay in the case of tritium concentrations). Atmospheric concentrations of sulfur hexafluoride have increased since the 1950s, and sulfur hexafluoride concentrations have been used to date recently recharged groundwater (Busenberg and Plummer, 2000). In addition, concentrations of tritium in precipitation (Michel, 1989) peaked in the 1960s and have been declining for the most part since that time; tritium concentrations were adjusted for radioactive decay to 2004 assuming a half-life of 12.3 years. A flux-weighted average concentration was calculated for each well by multiplying the concentration assigned to each particle by the amount of recharge associated with that particle and summing overall particles reaching a well. The calculated tracer concentrations derived from simulated flow paths and advective traveltimes were compared with measured concentrations and ages.

Table 7. Simulated water budget with inflow and outflow components to the local-scale modeled area.

Budget component	Inflow (cubic meters per day)	Outflow (cubic meters per day)	Net (cubic meters per day)	Net (cubic meters per second)
Drain	0	45,189.46	-45,189.46	-0.52
River leakage	10,612.05	32,054.86	-21,442.81	-.25
Recharge	79,756.98	0	79,756.98	.92
Specified boundary flows	59,574.94	50,875.85	8,699.09	.10
Multi-node wells	4,884.38	26,730.30	-21,845.92	-.25
Total:	154,828.34	154,850.47	-22.13	-.0026

Age Tracer Concentrations

Calculated sulfur hexafluoride concentrations were in good agreement with measured values in wells that were screened in the surficial aquifer system, intermediate confining unit, and in the top of the Upper Floridan aquifer. However, the agreement was not as good in wells open deeper in the Upper Floridan aquifer (fig. 20; table 8). For example, water from shallow monitoring well GARC-S23 (7 m deep) had a measured sulfur hexafluoride concentration of 5.27 pptv, whereas the calculated concentration was 5.65 pptv [pptv is the volume fraction, in parts per trillion, of sulfur hexafluoride in air that would be in equilibrium with the water sample in the recharge area, after adjustment for excess air (Busenberg and Plummer, 2000)]. The measured sulfur hexafluoride concentration was 0.23 pptv in water from monitoring well THC-F197 (60 m deep) and the calculated concentration was 1.31 pptv. Calculated concentrations do not match measured concentrations in deeper monitoring wells, probably because of uncertainty in the representation of karst features at that depth and the fact that deeper wells have longer flow paths. Also, the model probably does not exactly reflect the actual distribution of such features and the effects on flow paths. Measured sulfur hexafluoride concentration samples from the selected PSW ranged from 3.81 to 4.26 pptv, and the calculated value was 3.6 to 3.98 pptv (table 8).

Calculated tritium concentrations in the selected PSW from two separate sampling dates were about 2.5 and 2.4 tritium units (TU) and were slightly higher than the measured concentrations of about 2.2 and 2 TU (fig. 21; table 8). Many of the calculated concentrations of tritium for the surficial aquifer system and intermediate confining unit monitoring wells were similar to measured concentrations. For example, the measured tritium concentration in well 113RC-S35 was 2.15 TU, and the calculated concentration was 2.25 TU. Calculated tritium

concentrations were generally higher than measured concentrations in Upper Floridan aquifer wells, except for concentrations in those wells screened in the conduit layer in the Tampa Member, including the selected PSW (fig. 21). The measured tritium concentration was 0.04 TU in well GARC-F200 (open to the Upper Floridan aquifer), and the calculated concentration was 2.5 TU. In water from the deeper monitoring wells, the poor match between measured and calculated tritium concentrations may be a result of model limitations, such as inexact karst feature placement, the assumption of steady-state transport, and that a large percentage of the recharge water is older than tritium-age tracer data can be used for.

Simulated Particle Ages

Simulated particle ages representing the water recharging a well and derived from particle tracking cannot be compared directly with the apparent age of recharge water derived from the concentration of specific atmospheric tracers, such as sulfur hexafluoride and tritium, in groundwater. Atmospheric tracers yield an apparent age of recharge water for each well (Katz and others, 2007), whereas particle tracking yields an age distribution of water particles recharging each well. However, the apparent age from tracers can be compared to the median (or central tendency) of particle ages for each well to provide an assurance that the model provides reasonable traveltimes for water recharging wells and to give an approximation of land use in the area contributing recharge to each well at the time of recharge.

Simulated particle ages for monitoring wells ranged from less than 1 day to 99 years (table 9). Overall, particle ages agree favorably with apparent ages from atmospheric tracers for monitoring wells open to the surficial aquifer system and the intermediate confining unit, whereas the mixing of waters with a wide range of ages is less likely in wells open to the karstic Upper Floridan aquifer. The simulated and probable actual median particle ages generally increased with depth and hydrogeologic unit. The median simulated particle ages for all monitoring wells open to the surficial aquifer system (layers 1 to 3) was 1.9 years, but the ages ranged from less than 1 day to 9.5 years, whereas the apparent ages from atmospheric tracers ranged from 0 to 9 years (table 9). The median simulated particle age for monitoring wells screened in the intermediate confining unit ranged from 12.1 to 47.1 years; the maximum was 50.0 years (table 9). The apparent age for atmospheric tracers ranged from 0 to 14 years. The median ages of simulated particles for all monitoring wells open to the Tampa Member (layers 5 to 13, except for layer 8) was 24.3 years, but the medians ranged from 1.2 to 96 years (table 9). The apparent ages from atmospheric tracers ranged from 22 to 67 years. The oldest particle ages were simulated for monitoring well WP-F299, which was also the deepest well used in this study. The median of simulated particle ages for monitoring wells open to the conduit layer (model layer 8) was 14.9 years; the median particle ages ranged from 0.3 to 28.1 years. The apparent age from atmospheric tracers was 12 years.

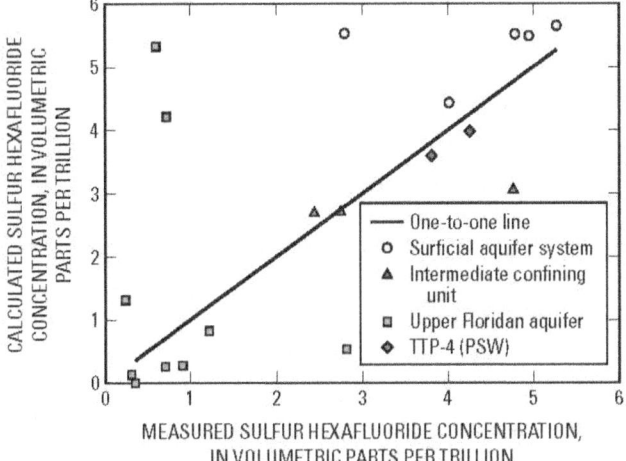

Figure 20. Calculated and measured sulfur hexafluoride concentrations in the selected public-supply well (PSW) and monitoring wells.

Table 8. Measured and simulated sulfur hexafluoride and tritium concentrations in the local-scale model and residual, weighted residual, and aquifer name for monitoring wells.

[Data source: Transport of Anthropogenic and Natural Contaminants (TANC). PSW is the selected public-supply well. UFA, Upper Floridan aquifer; ICU, intermediate confining unit; SAS, surficial aquifer system]

Short site name	Observed value	Simulated value	Residual	Weighted residual	Aquifer
Sulfur hexafluoride concentration, in volumetric parts per trillion					
113RC-F190	0.31	0.13	0.17	.0174	UFA
113RC-H50	2.44	2.68	-.24	-.77	ICU
113RC-S35	4.01	4.43	-.42	-1.33	SAS
GARC-F200	1.22	.82	.4	1.26	UFA
GARC-F75	.6	5.33	-4.73	-6.69	UFA
GARC-S23	5.27	5.65	-.38	-1.21	SAS
LP-H40	2.75	2.7	.0461	.15	ICU
LP-S30	2.8	5.53	-2.74	-8.66	SAS
RP-F103	.71	.25	.45	.72	UFA
RP-F77	.91	.27	.64	.91	UFA
RP-S20	4.78	5.52	-.74	-2.33	SAS
THC-F197	.23	1.31	-1.08	-3.42	UFA
THC-F75	.72	4.22	-3.49	-4.94	UFA
THC-SA/H46	4.76	3.06	1.71	5.4	SAS/ICU
WP-F150	2.81	.53	2.28	7.22	UFA
WP-F299	.34	0	.34	1.11	UFA
WP-S64	4.95	5.49	-.54	-1.72	SAS
TTP-4 (PSW)	3.81	3.6	.21	2.1	SAS
PSW AT 49 meters	4.26	3.98	.28	2.78	UFA
Tritium concentration, in tritium units					
113RC-F190	0.17	6.09	-5.91	-0.59	UFA
113RC-H50	1.33	1.85	-.52	-.52	ICU
113RC-S35	2.15	2.25	-.1	-.34	SAS
GARC-F200	.0400	2.5	-2.46	-1.74	UFA
GARC-F75	.43	1.87	-1.44	-1.02	UFA
GARC-S23	2.13	2	.13	.4	SAS
LP-H40	2.03	1.61	.42	1.33	ICU
LP-S30	2.58	1.78	.8	.57	SAS
RP-F103	.75	5.57	-4.82	-1.08	UFA
RP-F77	.74	5.37	-4.63	-1.04	UFA
RP-S20	2.22	1.94	.27	.86	SAS
THC-F197	.090	2.29	-2.2	-1.56	UFA
THC-F75	1.11	2.85	-1.74	-1.23	UFA
THC-SA/H46	2.48	2.04	.44	1.41	SAS/ICU
WP-F150	2.41	3.21	-.8	-2.54	UFA
WP-F299	0	.00954	-.095	.00954	UFA
WP-S64	2.59	1.93	.67	2.11	SAS
TTP-4 (PSW)	2.17	2.52	-.35	-3.53	SAS
TTP-4 (PSW) at 49 meters	1.99	2.4	-.41	-4.03	UFA

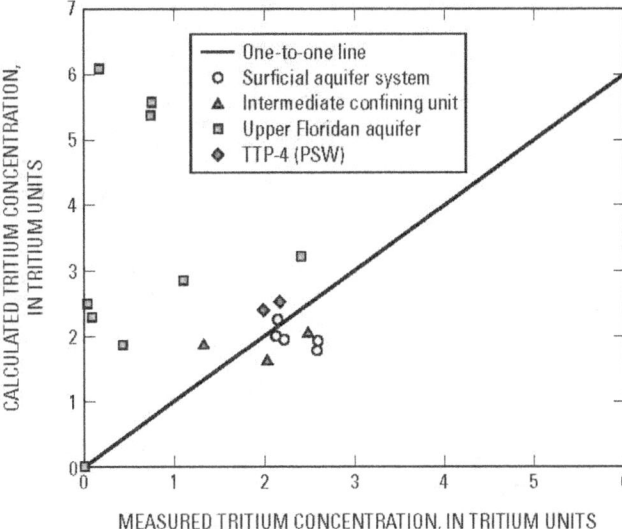

Figure 21. Calculated and measured tritium concentrations in the selected public-supply well (PSW) and monitoring wells.

Simulated particle ages ranged from less than 1 day to 127 years for the selected PSW, open in the conduit layer of the Upper Floridan aquifer, and nearly 45 percent of the simulated particle ages for the selected PSW were younger than about 10 years (table 9; fig. 22). The median simulated particle age for this well was 13.1 years; the average (from 11 samples) mean apparent age from sulfur hexafluoride was 9 years—the tritium age was not available for this well (table 9). Additional information on the mean apparent age of groundwater derived from age tracer concentrations is discussed in Katz and others (2007).

Comparison of Land Use in the Area Contributing Recharge and Occurrence of Selected Contaminants

The simulated ACR for the selected PSW encompasses about 24.3 km² and extends from 2.5 to 3 km north to northwest and 0.5 to 1.0 km south to southeast of the well (fig. 22). Although the simulated ACR for the selected PSW in Temple Terrace, Florida, likely does not represent the "true area contributing recharge," it is a useful tool for a general examination of current and past land uses at the time of recharge to approximate contaminants in groundwater recharging the PSW. The simulated ACR for the selected PSW is represented as a network of model-grid cells (some contiguous and others disconnected). The "patchy" appearance of the ACR, including the presence of areas of short-circuited flow paths and abbreviated traveltimes, is

Table 9. Simulated particle ages, minimum, median, and maximum at monitoring wells and at the selected public-suppy well compared to the apparent age of the young fraction of water, interpreted from sulfur hexafluoride and tritium concentrations by aquifer.

[<, less than; --, no data; ages in years, except where noted; shaded rows are wells that represent the conduit layer (layer 8) within the Upper Floridan aquifer]

Short site name	Particle (simulated) age			Measured apparent mean age of young fraction of water	
	Minimum	Median	Maximum	Sulfur hexa-fluoride	Tritium
Surficial aquifer system					
RP-S20	< 4 days	0.5	1.0	3	0
QRP-S20	.2	2.2	5.6	--	--
GARC-S23	< 1 day	< 8 days	< 11 days	2	9
LRP-S25	.9	.9	1.0	--	--
LP-S30	1.5	1.9	3.6	--	--
62SRP-S34	4.8	6.0	7 3	--	--
113RC-S35	2.0	4.3	9.5	7	4
BBP-S45	1.5	2.9	6.6	--	--
WP-S64	< 33 days	.7	1.3	4	5
Intermediate confining unit					
LP-H40	13.7	13.9	14.1	14	--
THC-SA-H46	6.6	12.1	12.6	4	0
113RC-H50	12.1	12.3	12.5	14	8
62SRSP-H55	11.8	13.9	16.6	--	--
LRP-H105	44.4	47.1	50.0	--	--
Upper Floridan aquifer					
MAS-R-F64	7.6	1.7	13.9	--	--
GARC-F75	1.2	1.2	1.2	27	33
THC-F75	5.5	6.0	6.6	25	29
RP-F77	32.4	32.4	32.4	23	22
RP-F103	33.2	33.2	33.2	25	29
WP-F150	20.5	28.1	42.6	12	12
LRP-F160	16.4	26.5	58.1	--	--
62SRP-F160	3.2	3.3	3.4	--	--
MAS-R-F160	.3	.3	16.2	--	--
TTP-4 (PSW)	< 1 day	13.1	127.0	5–10	--
113RC-F190	37.9	43.5	52.5	32	35
THC-F197	16.9	20.3	23.3	36	62
GARC-F200	20.4	24.3	29.1	30	67
WP-F299	91.3	96.3	99.1	31	--

Figure 22. Simulated area contributing recharge for the selected public-supply well (PSW) and age of particles derived from simulated particle traveltimes.

probably a realistic feature of this aquifer system. This finding is consistent with the conceptual understanding of the hydrogeology where some flow paths allow rapid flow through conduits and others allow slower flow through the relatively undisturbed matrix.

Current land use and land cover in the simulated ACR for the selected PSW are predominantly urban and residential (table 10). Based on recent land-use information (Homer and others, 2000), 84 percent of the ACR intersects residential/commercial land uses, followed by rangeland and wetland land covers, with a combined total of 10.6 percent. Only about 4 percent of the ACR intersects agricultural lands (table 9). Within the ACR urban/residential area, about 75 percent of the land use is residential (visually apparent on fig. 23) and the remaining 9 percent is commercial and barren land.

Table 10. Land-use statistics in the area contributing recharge area for the selected public-supply well, 2000.

Land-use category	Percent
Urban	83.73
Agriculture	4.43
Forest	.69
Rangeland	6.26
Barren	.11
Wetland	4.32
Water	.46
Total:	**100**

Mainly urban (industrial and gasoline derived) volatile organic compounds (VOCs), such as toluene and trichloroethylene (TCE), and lawn derived compounds, such as atrazine and nitrate contaminants, would be expected in the shallow groundwater beneath the ACR. The urban area was primarily developed in the late 1950s and 1960s with residential and commercial development replacing mostly agricultural or barren land. Land use in the ACR has remained relatively stable since that time. Nitrate and low concentrations of TCE, toluene, and atrazine and de-ethyl atrazine (degradation products of the triazine herbicides) are present in the selected PSW at levels above the expected background levels, but still below any drinking-water standards (Katz and others, 2007). Sources of nitrate are most likely from residential/commercial nitrogen fertilizer use and atmospheric deposition based on delta nitrogen-15/nitrogen-14 ($d^{15}N/^{14}N$) of nitrate (McMahon and others, 2008). The specific VOCs detected in the selected PSW are likely derived from urban land-use practices (Zogorski and others, 2006). Pesticides detected in the selected PSW could be derived from either agricultural or urban land use, but are most likely from urban land use in this area (Katz and others, 2007).

Simulated ACRs for the monitoring wells are also located mainly to the northwest and west, consistent with the conceptualization of the flow system in this area (fig. 24). Land use in the ACRs for the monitoring wells in the local-scale model area is similar to that of the selected PSW—mainly residential with a fraction of commercial and other land uses. Most samples from surficial aquifer system monitoring wells had nitrate concentrations that ranged from 0.21 to 6.11 mg/L as nitrogen. The average concentration of nitrate was 2.4 mg/L in monitoring wells screened in the surficial aquifer system. Typical VOCs in groundwater from urban land-use settings (trichloroethylene, tetrachloroethene, chloroform, and carbon disulfide) were found in most samples from surficial aquifer system wells. The pesticides atrazine, de-ethyl atrazine, and prometon were also found in six samples from the surficial aquifer system and intermediate confining unit wells and from three retention ponds, as discussed in Katz and others (2007). Generally, nitrate concentrations were lower in deeper monitoring wells than in the shallower monitoring wells. The median nitrate concentration was less than the detection level of 0.06 mg/L in most monitoring wells open to the Upper Floridan aquifer. Only the selected PSW and two other Upper Floridan aquifer wells (MAS-R-F160 and 62SRP-F160), open to the conduit layer in the Tampa Member (layer 8), had nitrate concentrations greater than the detection level.

Long-Term Concentrations of Nitrate in the Public-Supply Well

Groundwater is generally oxic in the surficial aquifer system, but conditions become anoxic near the interface between the surficial aquifer system and the intermediate confining unit, and into the Upper Floridan aquifer (Katz and others, 2007; McMahon and others, 2008); therefore, nitrate is transported conservatively through the surficial aquifer system. Near the interface within the intermediate confining unit and in the Upper Floridan aquifer, denitrification removes nitrate from groundwater, producing nitrogen gas and other byproducts of reactions (McMahon and others, 2008). Measured nitrate concentrations at the selected PSW ranged from 0.6 to 3.6 mg/L, which is consistent with recharge to this well from varying mixtures of young water from the surficial aquifer system that bypass denitrification processes and quickly recharge the well, and older deeper water from the Upper Floridan aquifer that is essentially nitrate free. Results from geochemical mass-balance mixing models for the selected PSW indicate that 50 to 70 percent of water withdrawn from this well is contributed from the surficial aquifer system, and 30 to 50 percent from the Upper Floridan aquifer (Katz and others, 2007). The selected PSW seems to be affected by the rapid downward movement (exacerbated by pumping) of contaminants from the surficial aquifer system to the well by means of sinkholes.

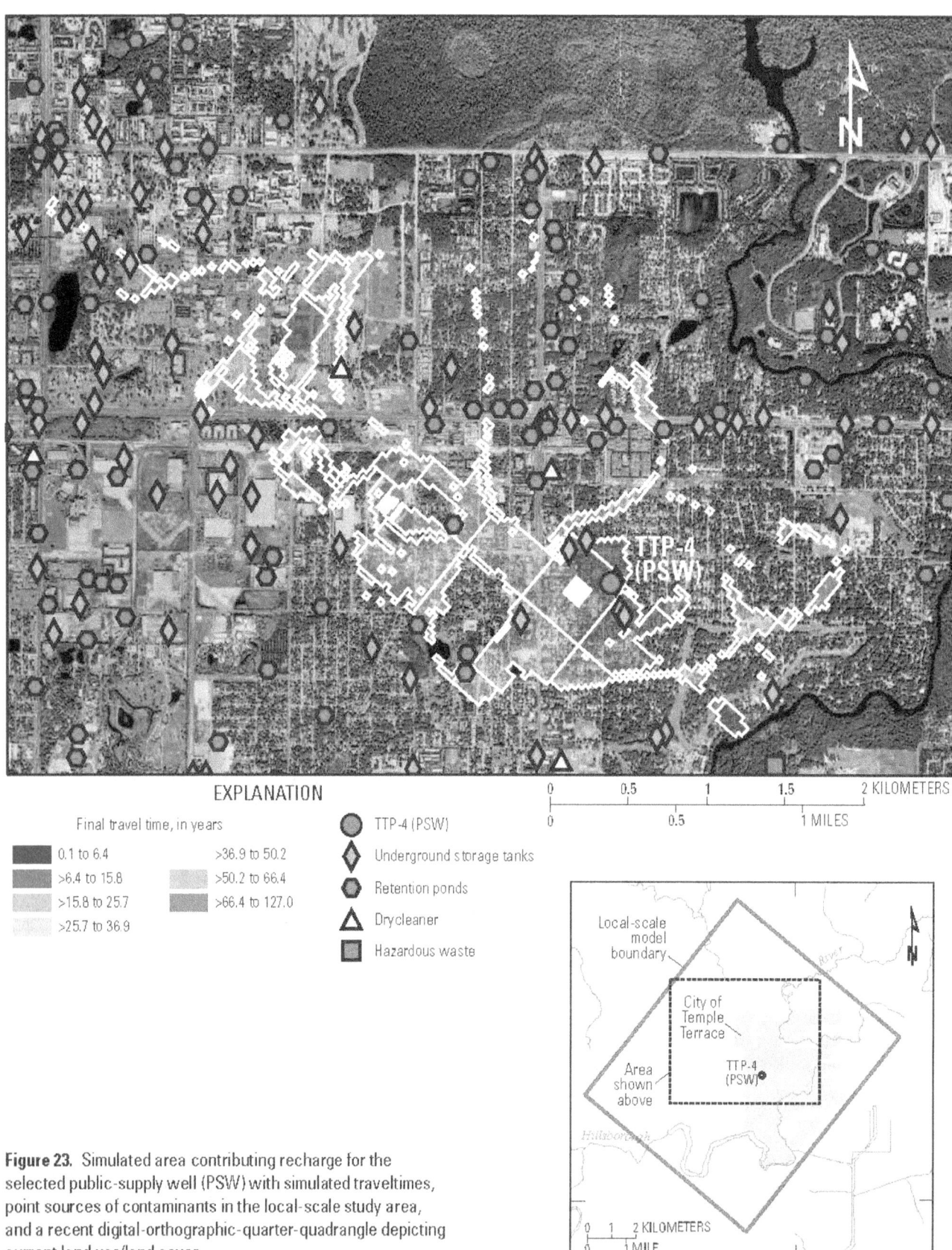

EXPLANATION

Final travel time, in years

0.1 to 6.4   >36.9 to 50.2

>6.4 to 15.8   >50.2 to 66.4

>15.8 to 25.7   >66.4 to 127.0

>25.7 to 36.9

TTP-4 (PSW)

Underground storage tanks

Retention ponds

Drycleaner

Hazardous waste

Figure 23. Simulated area contributing recharge for the selected public-supply well (PSW) with simulated traveltimes, point sources of contaminants in the local-scale study area, and a recent digital-orthographic-quarter-quadrangle depicting current land use/land cover.

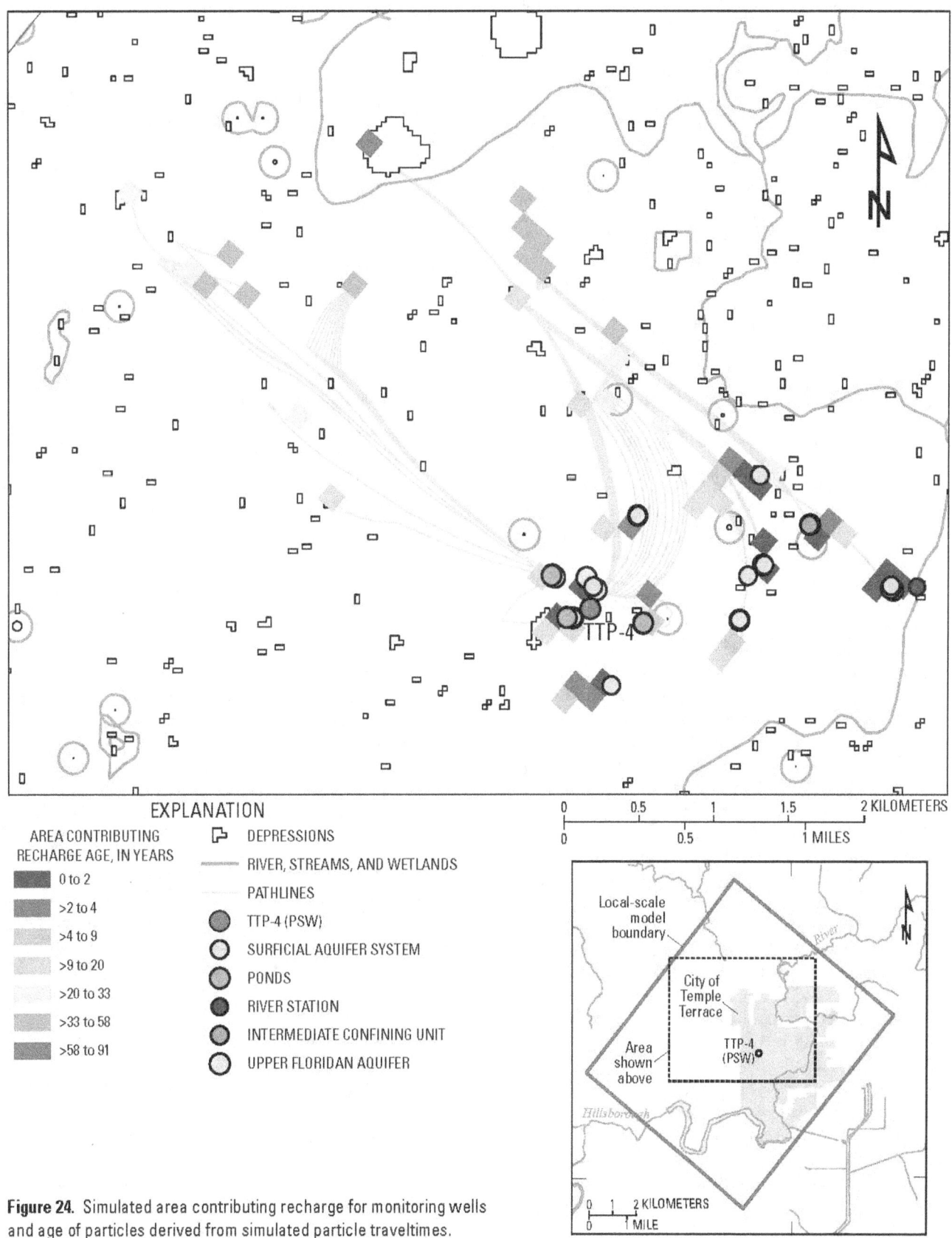

Figure 24. Simulated area contributing recharge for monitoring wells and age of particles derived from simulated particle traveltimes.

Long-term nitrate concentrations in the selected PSW will depend primarily on the quantity and timing of recharge events, withdrawals, land-use decisions, and concentrations of nitrate in the atmosphere over time within the ACR to the well. The nitrate concentration input history in local groundwater recharge was estimated by McMahon and others (2008) by summing measured nitrate and dissolved excess nitrogen gas (N_2) concentrations to obtain initial nitrate concentrations at the time of recharge. Denitrification rates were estimated using measured and initial nitrogen concentrations along with age tracer data. Estimated denitrification rates range from 0.1 to 0.5 mg/L as N per year in sediments below the surficial aquifer system within the local-scale model area.

Nitrate concentrations in the selected PSW were calculated over time as part of the present study by using an estimated nitrate concentration input history at the water table, based on sparse historically reported nitrate concentrations in water from wells in the local-scale model area and estimated reconstructed input concentrations from McMahon and others (2008). When available, a reported or reconstructed input value was used. When not available, however, the input was varied by using the nitrate concentrations from the surficial aquifer system and time of recharge data collected for this study. The nitrate input from 1900 to 1975 was estimated to be less than 0.84 mg/L as nitrogen (N). During 1975-92, the nitrate input was increased to 4.24 mg/L by using a linear slope of 0.1 mg/L per 6 months, based on the reconstructed input concentration for 1992. During 1992-2002, the estimated reconstructed nitrate input concentration varied temporally from 1.05 to 4.81 mg/L based on measured nitrate concentrations during that time period. The reconstructed nitrate input function for the selected PSW is shown in figure 25 along with measured values and estimated concentrations based on a range of denitrification rates. Variability in nitrate input concentrations are probably a more realistic way to simulate the input function because fertilizers are usually applied episodically, and whether or not nitrate reaches the water table also depends on the timing of recharge events, plant uptake, and other factors. Denitrification rates were also varied for each hydrogeologic unit based on given maximum, minimum, and mean values. Calculated nitrate concentrations in the selected PSW were estimated by using the same approach (flux weighted) as was used with sulfur hexafluoride and tritium comparisons with measured concentrations.

Input nitrate concentrations were flow weighted and tracked through model layers representing the different oxidation-reduction zones in the surficial aquifer system, intermediate confining unit, and Upper Floridan aquifer. Nitrate inputs were not modified, because particles were tracked through model layers 1 to 3, representing the oxic surficial aquifer system, where little or no denitrification is thought to occur (McMahon and others, 2008). As particles are tracked downward, reducing conditions begin near the interface within the intermediate confining unit and continue into the Upper Floridan aquifer (model layers 4 and greater). Median (0.3 per year), minimum, and maximum rates, applied

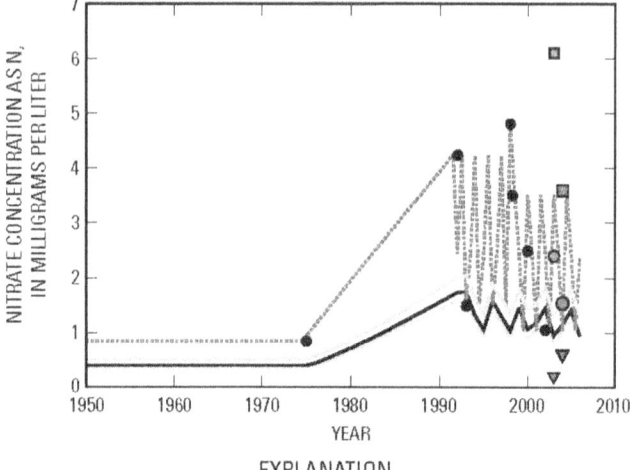

EXPLANATION

---- Simulated nitrate concentration in the selected PSW using 0.5 milligrams per liter as N per year denitrification rate

—— Simulated nitrate concentration in the selected PSW using 0.3 milligrams per liter as N per year denitrification rate

-·-·-·- Modified reconstructed INPUT nitrate concentration function

Simulated nitrate concentration in the selected PSW using 0.5 milligrams per liter as N per year denitrification rate

OBSERVED NITRATE CONCENTRATION

- ◎ Mean in selected PSW for 2003 and 2004
- ▽ Minimum in selected PSW in 2003 and 2004
- ▣ Maximum in selected PSW in 2003 and 2004
- ◉ Mean in surficial aquifer system wells in 2003 and 2004
- ▼ Minimum in surficial aquifer system wells in 2003 and 2004
- ▪ Maximum in surficial aquifer system wells in 2003 and 2004
- ● Reconstructed nitrate concentrations, from McMahon and others (2008)

Figure 25. Estimated nitrate input concentrations, reconstructed nitrate in recharge concentrations, estimated nitrate concentrations at the selected public-supply well (PSW) from flow-weighted particle tracking using median, minimum, and maximum denitrification rates, and measured nitrate concentrations at the selected PSW and surficial aquifer system wells sampled in 2003 and 2004.

to the flow-weighted nitrate input concentrations, were assumed for particles as they were tracked from the water table to the selected PSW. The final calculated nitrate concentration at the selected PSW over time is given as the sum of flow-weighted nitrate concentrations of all particles reaching the selected PSW for each year.

The final nitrate concentration calculated for the selected PSW agreed relatively well with measured values and varied with the input function over time (figs. 25 and 26). Because the input history is somewhat uncertain over time, this study focuses mainly on the distribution of calculated concentrations from 1992 to 2006, where there are more reconstructed nitrate input data for the recharging waters. Also, land use was relatively stable over this period. Final calculated nitrate concentrations in the selected PSW varied from 0.80 to 2.05 mg/L with a median and mean concentration of 1.33 and

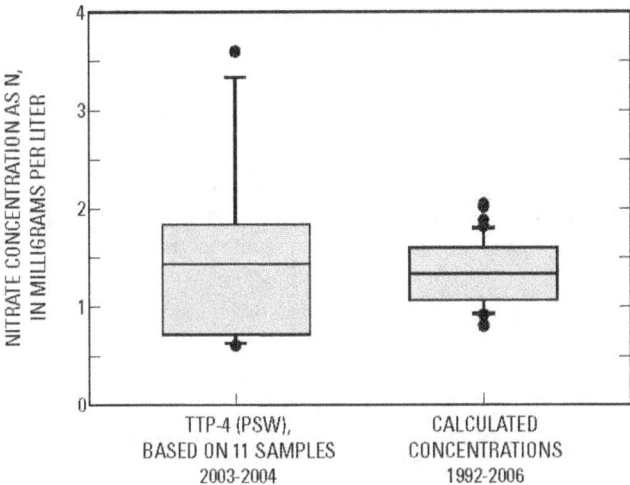

Figure 26. Nitrate concentrations in the selected public-supply well (PSW) sampled in 2003 and 2004 compared to calculated concentrations from 1992 to 2006.

1.36 mg/L, respectively. The median nitrate concentration from water samples collected in 2003 and 2004 from the selected PSW was 1.44 mg/L, and the average concentration was 1.54 mg/L—slightly higher than the calculated concentrations (fig. 26). The range in nitrate concentrations (0.61 to 3.6 mg/L) from water samples from the selected PSW was greater than the range of calculated values, but the central tendencies are represented relatively well. This may indicate that the input function does not vary enough in time and (or) space to adequately represent the true variability of nitrate concentrations in recharge water entering the groundwater flow system. Also, calculated concentrations likely will not match measured concentrations exactly, because the groundwater flow model represents steady-state conditions and does not simulate individual recharge or fertilizer application episodes. For comparison, compliance concentrations of nitrate reported for the blended treated water samples from Temple Terrace selected PSWs from 1999 to 2001 ranged from 1.2 to 2.4 mg/L (based on calculated values and four samples). Assuming that recent (1990s and later) land-use activities remain relatively constant over time, nitrate concentrations in the selected PSW will likely remain relatively constant for the foreseeable future and will remain well below the maximum contaminant level for nitrate of 10 mg/L as nitrogen.

The vulnerability of the selected PSW to nonpoint source inputs of nitrate, pesticides, and (or) other contaminants, such as VOCs, is evident from the water chemistry data (Katz and others, 2007) and the nitrate calculations presented in this report. Assuming that present groundwater flow conditions persist into the future, long-term concentrations of nitrate and VOCs and pesticides in the selected PSW will depend on the input of contaminants at the water table and recharge events in the future.

The calculated long-term nitrate concentrations in the selected PSW also reflect a difference of 1 to 10 years between peak input concentrations and peak concentrations in the well. This apparent timelag between input concentrations over time and the resulting concentrations in the well are the result of the wide range of ages of water reaching the selected PSW, the variability in input over time, and denitrification rates. An understanding of the length of time between changes in input concentrations and resulting concentrations in the selected PSW is needed to predict the impact of changes in land-use management.

To the extent that the conditions affecting the vulnerability of the selected PSW are typical of conditions affecting other selected PSWs in the region, these results can be useful in evaluating the vulnerability of other wells to nonpoint source input of contaminants. Patchy high nitrate concentrations have been observed in shallow groundwater beneath urban land throughout the regional-scale study area. About 75 percent of the public-supply wells in the regional study area with open intervals beginning at depths similar to the selected PSW may be similarly impacted by nitrate, pesticides, and VOC concentrations. Public supply wells with high pumping rates, open intervals at shallow depths, and in close proximity to karst features may receive appreciable flows of young water that would likely have higher concentrations of nitrate, pesticides, and VOCs, because these wells will likely have less mixing with old water containing low contaminant concentrations.

Summary and Conclusions

In 2002, a single public-supply well, TTP-4, was selected for intensive study to evaluate the dominant processes affecting the vulnerability of public-supply wells in the Tampa Bay region, Florida. A network of 29 monitoring wells was installed to support a detailed analysis of physical and chemical conditions and processes affecting the water chemistry of the selected public-supply well (PSW). A three-dimensional, steady-state groundwater flow model was developed for this study to evaluate the age of groundwater reaching the well and to test hypotheses on the vulnerability of the selected PSW to nonpoint sources of contaminants. The local-scale model is nested within the steady-state regional model and was calibrated for calendar year 2000. The local-scale model was discretized into a uniform grid of finite-difference cells with 80 rows and 69 columns of 125 meters length on a side. The local-scale model grid has 13 layers of variable thickness. The active area of the model coincides with the water table at the top of the model and the bottom of the regional-scale model layer 13, which is below the bottom of the PSW and below the dominant pumping zone in the local-scale model area.

The regional-scale model was used to specify stresses in the local-scale model, including specified flow on model boundaries and groundwater withdrawals. Recharge rates in the local-scale model ranged from a base value of 25.6 up to 1,610.2 centimeters per year (in one cell) of the model grid. Recharge was increased where karst features (closed-basin depressions) were known or thought to be present. Lateral boundaries in the local-scale model were derived from the regional-scale model with specified fluxes assigned to boundary cells. Withdrawals from public-supply wells were determined from reported permitted average withdrawal rates in the year 2000—relatively stable for this area. Withdrawal rates for agricultural and industrial wells were based on previous studies.

The flow system is composed of the surficial aquifer system, intermediate confining unit, and freshwater part of the Upper Floridan aquifer representing sand, clay, and limestone and dolostone, respectively. The model was calibrated using systematic manual calibration techniques, MODFLOW-2000, and finally UCODE parameter estimation techniques. The hydraulic and other parameters that were used, including recharge, anisotropy, and porosity, were modified until a best fit solution to hydraulic heads, hydraulic gradients, and age tracer concentrations was achieved for groundwater flow and subsequent particle tracking simulations and tracer concentration calculations.

Particle tracking was used to compute flow paths and advective traveltimes in the model area. The computed area contributing recharge (ACR) for the selected PSW covered about 24.3 square kilometers, extending from about 0.5 to 1.0 kilometers to the south and southeast of the well to about 2.5 to 3 kilometers to the north and northwest of the well, underlying a predominantly urban residential land-use area. The simulated ages of particles reaching the selected PSW ranged from 1 day to 127.0 years with a median of 13.1 years.

Groundwater older than about 80 years within the ACR would be expected to contain primarily agricultural or related contaminants, whereas groundwater younger than 80 years would be expected to contain both urban and agricultural contaminants since urban development began to fill in the local-scale model area in the 1950s. Elevated concentrations of nitrate and low concentrations of volatile organic compounds and pesticides were observed in water from the selected PSW, which is consistent with mainly urban sources.

Nitrate concentrations in the ACR to the selected PSW are highest in shallow groundwater. The median nitrate concentration in wells open to the surficial aquifer system beneath the urban area was 2.4 mg/L (milligrams per liter). Groundwater is generally oxic in the surficial aquifer system; therefore, nitrate is expected to be transported conservatively through that part of the system. Nitrate concentrations decreased with depth to background concentrations of less than 0.06 mg/L in monitoring wells screened in the Upper Floridan aquifer due to denitrification in the intermediate confining unit and Upper Floridan aquifer. Denitrification rates varied between 0.1 and 0.5 mg/L as N per year.

The nitrate concentration in the selected PSW (median 1.44 mg/L) is intermediate between the shallow and deep parts of the zone of contribution because of mixing of relatively young and older groundwater at the well. Because of the rapid and dominant downward movement of water in the local-scale model area through sinkholes exacerbated by pumping, nitrate in shallow groundwater in the surficial aquifer system is expected to continue to reach the selected PSW with time. Estimated nitrate concentrations in recharge over time, represented by using observed nitrate concentrations and corresponding groundwater recharge dates, indicate overall relatively steady concentrations of nitrate in recharge over time in the area contributing recharge. Assuming that the proportion of urban land use remains fixed at the current proportion of 84 percent urban land use and input concentrations beneath these settings remain relatively constant, calculated long-term nitrate concentrations in the selected PSW indicate that concentrations will continue to be about 1 to 3 mg/L for the foreseeable future. The calculated long-term nitrate concentrations in the selected PSW also indicate a 1- to 10-year timelag between changes in input concentrations in groundwater recharge and resulting concentrations in the well. An understanding of the length of time between changes in input concentrations and resulting concentrations in the selected PSW is needed to predict the impact of changes in land use.

References Cited

Anderson, M.P., and Woessner, W.W., 1992, Applied groundwater modeling: San Diego, Academic Press, 381 p.

Böhlke, J.K., Mroczkowski, S.J., and Coplen, T.B., 2003, Oxygen isotopes in nitrate: New reference materials for 18O:17O:16O measurements and observations on nitrate-water equilibration: Rapid Communications in Mass Spectrometry, v. 17, p. 1835-1846.

Busenberg E., and Plummer, L.N., 2000, Dating young ground water with sulfur hexafluoride: Natural and anthropogenic sources of sulfur hexafluoride: Water Resources Research, v. 36, no. 10, p. 3011-3030.

Bush, P.W., and Johnston, R.H., 1988, Ground-water hydraulics, regional flow, and ground-water development of the Upper Floridan aquifer in Florida and in parts of Georgia, South Carolina, and Alabama: U.S. Geological Survey Professional Paper 1403-C, 80 p.

Carr, W.J., and Alverson, D.C., 1959, Stratigraphy of middle Tertiary rocks in part of west-central Florida: U.S. Geological Survey Bulletin 1092, p. 1-109.

City of Temple Terrace, 2006, City of Temple Terrace history: Available online at *http://www.templeterrace.com/misc/history_index.htm*

Coffin, J.E., and Fletcher, W.L., 2001, Water-resources data, Florida, water year 2000: U.S. Geological Survey Water-Data Report FL-00-3A, 359 p.

Crandall, C.A., 2007, Hydrogeologic setting and ground-water flow simulations of the Northern Tampa Bay regional study area, Florida, *Section 5 of* Paschke, S.S. ed., Hydrogeologic settings and ground-water flow simulations for regional studies of the transport of anthropogenic and natural contaminants to public-supply wells: U.S. Geological Survey Professional Paper 1737-A, p. 5-1 to 5-30. Available online at *http://pubs.usgs.gov/pp/2007/1737a/Section5.pdf*

Culbreath, M.A, 1988, Geophysical investigation of lineaments in south Florida: Master's thesis: Tampa, Department of Geology, University of South Florida, 97 p.

Domenico, P.A., and Schwartz, F.W., 1990, Physical and chemical hydrogeology: New York, John Wiley, 824 p.

Eberts, S.M., Erwin, M.L., and Hamilton, P.A., 2005, Assessing the vulnerability of public-supply wells to contamination from urban, agricultural, and natural sources: U.S. Geological Survey Fact Sheet 2005-3022, 4 p.

Farnsworth, R.K., Thompson, E.S., and Peck, E.L., 1982, Evaporation atlas for the contiguous 48 United States: Asheville, N.C., National Oceanic and Atmospheric Administration Technical Report NWS 33, 26 p., 4 sheets.

Fernandez, M., Jr., Goetz, C.L., and Miller, J.E., 1984, Evaluation of future base-flow water-quality conditions in the Hillsborough River, Florida: U.S. Geological Survey Water-Resources Investigations Report 83-4182, 47 p.

Florida Department of Environmental Protection, 2003, The Land Boundary Information System (Labins): Tallahassee, Division of State Lands, Bureau of Survey and Mapping. Available online at *http://data.labins.org/2003/index.cfm*

Focazio, M.J., Reilly, T.E., Rupert, M.G., and Helsel, D.R., 2002, Assessing ground-water vulnerability to contamination: Providing scientifically defensible information for decision makers: U.S. Geological Survey Circular 1224, 33 p.

Franke, O.L., Reilly, T.E., Pollock, D.W., and LaBaugh, J.W., 1998, Estimating areas contributing recharge to wells: Lessons from previous studies: U.S. Geological Survey Circular 1174, 14 p.

Goetz, C.L., Reichenbaugh, R.C., and Ogle, J.K., 1978, Water-supply potential of the lower Hillsborough River, 1976: U.S. Geological Survey Water-Resources Investigations 78-29, 25 p.

Halford, K.J., and Hanson, R.T., 2002, User guide for the drawdown-limited, Multi-Node Well (MNW) Package for the U.S. Geological Survey's modular three-dimensional finite-difference ground-water flow model, versions MODFLOW-96 and MODFLOW-2000: U.S. Geological Survey Open-File Report 02-293, 39 p.

Harbaugh, A.W., Banta, E.R., Hill, M.C., and McDonald, M.G., 2000, MODFLOW-2000, The U.S. Geological Survey modular ground-water model—User guide to modularization concepts and the ground-water flow process: U.S. Geological Survey Open-File Report 00-92, 121 p.

Homer, Collin, Huang, Chengquan, Yang, Limin, and Wylie, Bruce, 2000, Development of a circa 2000 landcover database for the United States: Web paper under U.S. Geological Survey contract 1434-CR-97-CN-40274 with Raytheon Corporation, Sioux Falls, S. Dak., 13 p., Available online at *http://landcover.usgs.gov/pdf/asprs_final.pdf*

Hutson, S.S., Barber, N.L., Kenny, J.F., Linsey, K.S., Lumia, D.S., and Maupin, M.A., 2004, Estimated use of water in the United States in 2000: U.S. Geological Survey Circular 1268, 46 p.

HydroGeoLogic, Inc., 1997, Development of a computer model of the regional groundwater flow system in Hernando County Water Resources Assessment Project, Phase I—Data compilation and analysis: Brooksville, Report on file at the Southwest Florida Water Management District, variously paged.

Katz, B.G., Crandall, C.A., Metz, P.A., McBride, W.S., and Berndt, M.P., 2007, Chemical characteristics, water sources and pathways, and age distribution of ground water in the contributing area of a public-supply well near Tampa, Florida, 2002-05: U.S. Geological Survey Scientific Investigations Report 2007-5139, 85 p.

Kauffman, L.J., Stackelberg, P.E., and Ayers, M.A., 1998, Simulation of advective transport of nonpoint source contaminants in an unconfined aquifer: 1998 Fall Meeting Abstract Supplement, Dec. 6-10, 1998, San Francisco, Calif.: EOS, Transactions of the American Geophysical Union, v. 79, no. 45, p. F314.

Knochenmus, L.A., and Robinson, J.L., 1996, Descriptions of anisotropy and heterogeneity and their effect on ground-water flow and areas of contribution to public-supply wells in a karst carbonate aquifer system: U.S. Geological Survey Water-Supply Paper 2475, 43 p.

Langevin, C.D., 1998, Stochastic methods for evaluating the potential for wetland rehydration in covered-karst terranes: Tampa, University of South Florida, Ph.D. dissertation, 133 p.

Leake, S.A., and Claar, D.V., 1999, Procedures and computer programs for telescopic mesh refinement using MODFLOW: U.S. Geological Survey Open-File Report 99-238, 53 p.

Lewelling, B.R., 2004, Extent of areal inundation of riverine wetlands along five river systems in the upper Hillsborough River watershed, west-central Florida: U.S. Geological Survey Scientific Investigations Report 2004-5133, 43 p.

Marella, R.L., and Berndt, M.P., 2005, Water withdrawals and trends from the Upper Floridan aquifer in the southeastern United States, 1950-2000: U.S. Geological Survey Circular 1278, 20 p.

Maupin, M.A., and Barber, N.L., 2005, Estimated withdrawals from principal aquifers in the United States, 2000: U.S. Geological Survey Circular 1279, 46 p.

McMahon, P.B., Böhlke, J.K., Kauffman, L.J., Kipp, K.L, Landon, M.K., Crandall, C.A., Burow, K.R., and Brown, C.J., 2008, Source and transport controls on the movement of nitrate to public supply wells in selected principal aquifers of the United States: Water Resources Research, v. 44, ww04401, doi:10.1029/2007, WR006252.

Michel, R.M., 1989, Tritium deposition in the continental United States, 1953-1983: U.S. Geological Survey Water-Resources Investigations Report 89-4072, 46 p.

Miller, J.A., 1986, Hydrogeologic framework of the Upper Floridan aquifer: U.S. Geological Survey Professional Paper 1403-B, 91 p.

Murphy, W.R., Jr., 1978, Flood-profiles for Cypress Creek, west-central Florida: U.S. Geological Survey Water-Resources Investigations Report 78-8, 29 p.

Owenby, J.R., and Ezell, D.S., 1992, Monthly station normals of temperature, precipitation, and heating and cooling degree days, 1961-1990, Florida: Asheville, U.S. Department of Commerce National Oceanic and Atmospheric Administration, National Climatic Data Center, 28 p.

Poeter, E.P., Hill, M.C., Banta, E.R., Mehl, S., and Christensen, S., 2005, UCODE_2005 and six other computer codes for universal sensitivity analysis, calibration, and uncertainty evaluation: U.S. Geological Survey Techniques and Methods, Book 6. chap. 11, sec. A, p. 283.

Pollack, D.W., 1994, User's guide for MODPATH/MODPATH-PLOT, version 3: A particle tracking post-processing package for MODFLOW: The U.S. Geological Survey finite-difference ground-water flow model: U.S. Geological Survey Open-File Report 94-464, 248 p.

Reilly, T.E., 2001, System and boundary conceptualization in ground-water flow simulation: Applications of hydraulics: U.S. Geological Survey Techniques of Water Resources Investigations, Book 3, chap. B8, 29 p.

Ryder, P.D., 1985, Hydrology of the Upper Floridan aquifer in west-central Florida: U.S. Geological Survey Professional Paper 1403-F, 63 p.

Schmidt, W., 1994, Florida's geological history and geological resources: Tallahassee, Florida Geological Survey Special Publication 35, 66 p.

SDI Environmental Services, Inc., 1997, Water resources evaluation and integrated hydrologic model of the northern Tampa Bay region: Clearwater, Fla., Consultant's report in the files of Tampa Bay Water, 146 p.

Sepulveda, Nicasio, 2002, Simulation of ground-water flow in the intermediate and Upper Floridan aquifers in peninsular Florida: U.S. Geological Survey Water-Resources Investigations Report 02-4009, 130 p.

Sinclair, W.C., 1974, Hydrogeologic characteristics of the surficial aquifer in northwest Hillsborough County, Florida: Tallahassee, Florida Bureau of Geology Information Circular 86, 98 p.

Stackelberg, P.E., Kauffman, L.J., Baehr, A.L., and Ayers, M.A., 2000, Comparison of nitrate, pesticides, and volatile organic compounds in samples from monitoring and public-supply wells, Kirkwood-Cohansey aquifer system, southern New Jersey: U.S. Geological Survey Water-Resources Investigations Report 00-4123, 51 p.

Stewart, J.W., Goetz, C.L., and Mills, L.R., 1978, Hydrogeology factors affecting the availability and quality of ground water in the Temple Terrace area, Hillsborough County, Florida: U.S. Geological Survey Water-Resources Investigations 78-4, 38 p.

Stoker, Y.E., Levesque, V.A., and Woodham, W.M., 1996, The effects of discharge and water quality of the Alafia River, Hillsborough River, and the Tampa Bypass Canal on nutrient loading to Hillsborough Bay, Florida: U.S. Geological Survey Water-Resources Investigation Report 95-4107, 69 p.

Trommer, J.T., 1987, Potential for pollution of the Upper Floridan aquifer from five sinkholes and an internally drained basin in west-central Florida: U.S. Geological Survey Water-Resources Investigations Report 87-4013, 103 p.

Turner, J.F., 1974, Flood profiles of the lower Hillsborough River, Florida: U.S. Geological Survey Open-File Report FL-74003, 29 p.

White, W.A., 1970, Geomorphology of the Florida peninsula: Tallahassee, Florida Bureau of Geology Bulletin 51, 164 p.

Williams, S.R., 1985, Relationship of ground water chemistry to photolineaments in a karst aquifer: Tampa, Geology Department, University of South Florida, M.S. Thesis.

Wolansky, R.M., and Thompson, T.H., 1987, Relation between ground water and surface water in the Hillsborough River basin, west-central Florida: U.S. Geological Survey Water-Resources Investigations Report 87-4010, 58 p.

Yobbi, D.K., 2000, Application of nonlinear least-squares regression to ground-water flow modeling, west-central Florida: U.S. Geological Survey Water-Resources Investigations Report 00-4094, 58 p.

Zogorski, J.S., Carter, J.M., Ivahnenko, T., Lapham, W.W., Moran, M.J., Rowe, B.L., Squillace, P.J., Toccalino, P.L., 2006, Volatile organic compounds in the Nation's ground water and drinking water supply wells: U.S. Geological Survey Circular 1292, 101 p.

Appendix References

Crandall, C.A., 2007, Hydrogeologic setting and ground-water flow simulations of the Northern Tampa Bay regional study A=area, Florida, *Section 5 of* Paschke, S.S. ed., Hydrogeologic settings and ground-water flow simulations for regional studies of the transport of anthropogenic and natural contaminants to public-supply wells: U.S. Geological Survey Professional Paper 1737-A, p. 5-1 to 5-30. Available online at *http://pubs.usgs.gov/pp/2007/1737a/Section5.pdf*

Harbaugh, A.W., Banta, E.R., Hill, M.C., and McDonald, M.G., 2000, MODFLOW-2000, The U.S. Geological Survey modular ground-water model—User guide to modularization concepts and the ground-water flow process: U.S. Geological Survey Open-File Report 00-92, 121 p.

Appendix

The regional ground-water flow model, documented in Crandall (2007), was updated and optimized using parameter estimation in MODFLOW 2000 to improve recharge estimates in the local-scale model area, because this model was used to develop boundary conditions along the local-scale TANC model boundary. Hydraulic conductivity and recharge parameters were optimized by lumping similar zones to reduce the number of parameters and to eliminate correlation problems. The following figures present the final updated values for horizontal hydraulic conductivity for the Upper Floridan aquifer (fig. A-1) vertical hydraulic conductivity of the Upper Floridan aquifer (fig. A-2); the updated recharge optimized values (fig. A 3); and the horizontal hydraulic conductivity for the surficial aquifer system (fig. A-4).

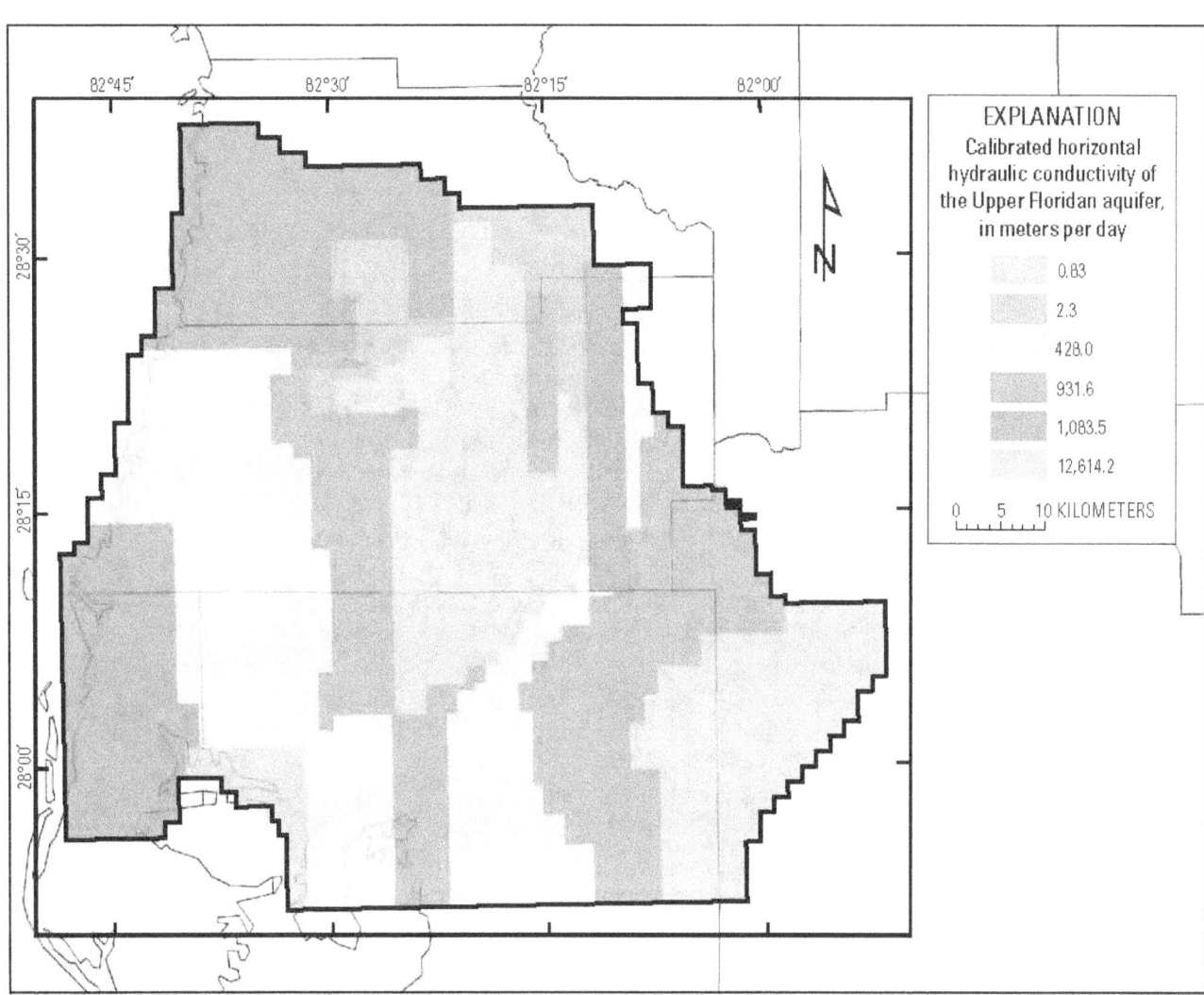

Figure A-1. Updated estimates of horizontal hydraulic conductivity of the Upper Floridan aquifer for the regional model that was used to estimate flow at the boundary of the local-scale model.

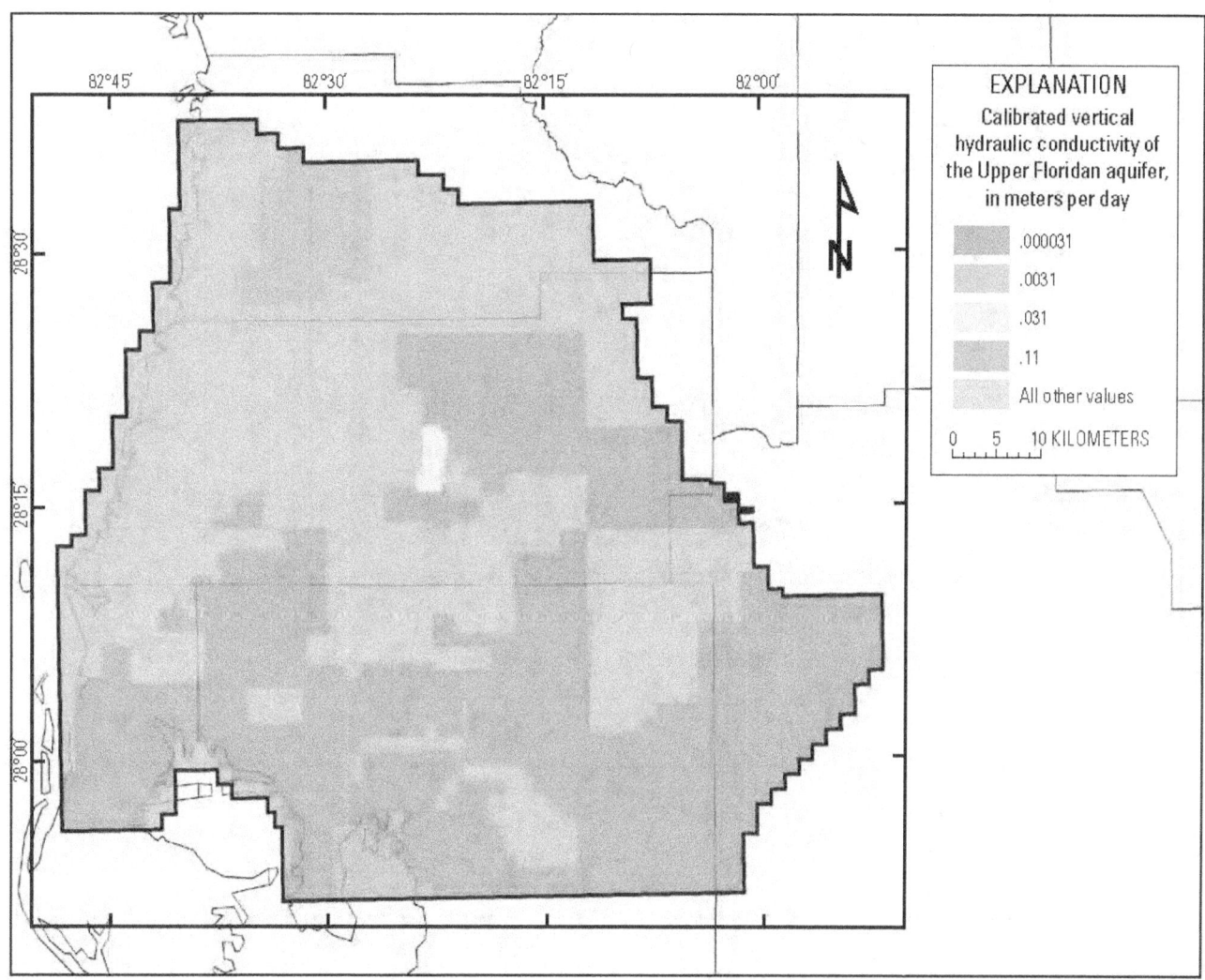

Figure A-2. Updated estimates of vertical hydraulic conductivity of the Upper Floridan aquifer for the regional model that was used to estimate flow at the boundary of the local-scale model.

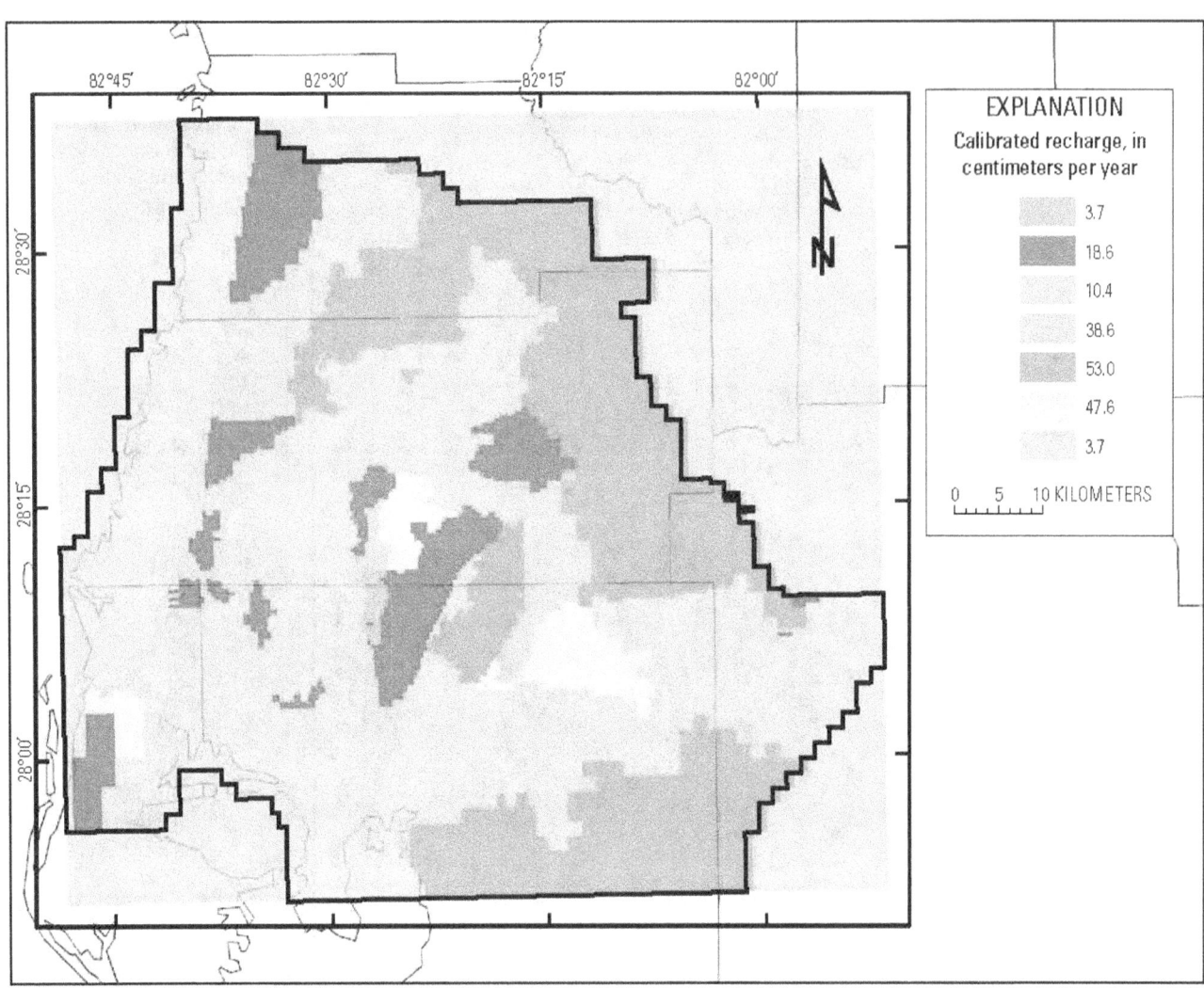

Figure A-3. Updated estimates of recharge for the regional model that was used to estimate flow at the boundary of the local-scale model.

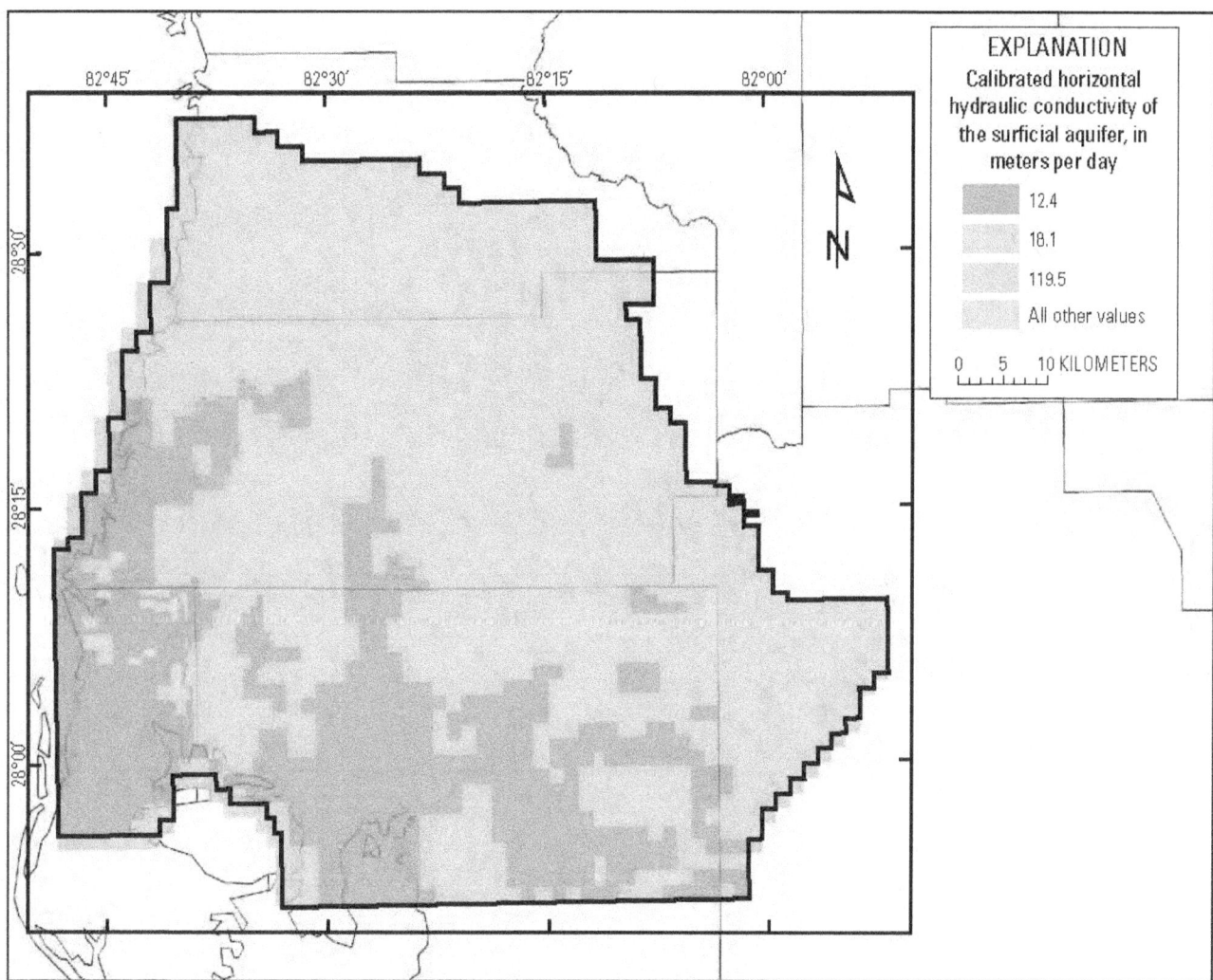

Figure A-4. Updated estimates of horizontal hydraulic conductivity for the surficial aquifer (layer 1) in the regional model that was used to estimate flow at the boundary of the local-scale model.